AF508183

Unfinished Business

30 Sips of Faith, Words, and Wisdom for Life's Messy Middle

© 2026 The Learning Doctor Consulting LLC.
All rights reserved.

No part of this publication may be reproduced, distributed, or transmitted in any form or by any means, including photocopying, recording, or other electronic or mechanical methods, without the prior written permission of the publisher, except as permitted by U.S. copyright law. For permission requests, contact The Learning Doctor Consulting, LLC; thelearningdr105@gmail.com.

First edition March 2026

Illustrations: Veronica Walton

Interior and cover design: Raquel Colmenares

ISBN: 979-8-9941600-1-5

Scripture quotations taken from The Holy Bible, New International Version®, NIV®. Copyright © 1973, 1978, 1984, 2011 by Biblica, Inc. Used with permission of Zondervan. All rights reserved worldwide. www.zondervan.com

The habit framework used in this devotional is inspired by the Tiny Habits framework developed by BJ Fogg, PhD, as described in Tiny Habits: The Small Changes That Change Everything (Houghton Mifflin Harcourt, 2019). "Tiny Habits®" is a trademark of BJ Fogg.

UNFINISHED BUSINESS

30 Sips of Faith, Words, and Wisdom for Life's Messy Middle

SHANTEL M. SCOTT, ED.D.

A Little Note From Your Future Favorite Author

Sometimes life throws a curveball, or maybe you wake up one morning and wonder, is this it? If that thought feels familiar, take this as your invitation to level up. Not tomorrow, not someday soon, but right here, right now, as you turn these pages. Welcome to your 30-day journey toward becoming your best self.

So, What's a #BestSelfie Life, Anyway?

Forget the perfect filters and the meticulously curated social media feeds. This isn't about looking good; it's about being good to yourself, to others, and most importantly, to God. It's a daily, intentional practice, wrapped in these powerful letters:

S – Stopping: Hit the brakes. Seriously. Step off the hustle, the worry-go-round, the endless to-do list that stresses you out just by existing. Stop. Breathe.

E – Erasing the Negativity: Actively, defiantly, choose to let go of the doubt, the fear, the exhausting comparisons, and those worn-out limiting beliefs. Clear the slate. You deserve a fresh start.

L – Looking Around: Open your eyes. See the blessings, the unexpected beauty, and the lessons staring you in the face. They've been there all along, waiting for you to notice.

F – Finding Joy in What Is: Practice gratitude for the glorious mess of your life right now. Embrace the imperfect, the unfinished, and the small, everyday gifts. Stop chasing the "next big thing" and savor the "this big moment."

I – Inhaling: Breathe in God's peace, His presence, His power, His promises. This isn't just air, it's faith. Let it fill you.

E – Exhaling: Release. Let go of the burdens, the anxieties, the illusion of control (because let's be honest, you don't have it anyway). Breathe out trust. Let it flow.

This isn't just a clever acronym; it's a blueprint for living authentically, for living a life that shines. And it's rooted in the wisdom of a man who lives it daily: my dad.

My OG of Goodness: Rev

For most of my life, I've had the ultimate cheat code: a front-row seat to a masterclass in living well. That masterclass comes courtesy of my father, the man you're about to meet as Rev. He isn't just a source of wisdom or a figure of authority; he is the living, breathing embodiment of a faith that doesn't just weather storms—it thrives in them. I've seen him face challenges that might send most of us spiraling into a Netflix binge, yet he meets them with unshakable peace and a quiet strength that borders on superhero status. By sheer example, he taught me that faith isn't some quaint Sunday ritual. It's not about being perfect; it's about leaning on something bigger, living with intention, and carrying a joy that's almost impossible not to catch.

But here's the thing: what truly sets him apart is his effortless embodiment of the fruits of the Spirit. His love overflows. His joy runs like a quiet current, steady even in the rough moments. His peace? Tangible. He shows patience, kindness, and goodness in every interaction. His faithfulness never wavers, his gentleness soothes, and his self-control reflects a spirit anchored in discipline. To witness it isn't just inspiring, it's transformative.

My Own Beautifully Messy Journey

That all sounds amazing, but the truth is, even with a VIP pass to greatness, living like Rev hasn't always been easy. I'd be lying if I said I always understood. There were plenty of times I thought I knew better, or that his so-called "old-school" wisdom couldn't possibly apply to my modern dilemmas. Spoiler alert: it always did. Especially when you hit your forties and those curveballs stop feeling playful and start landing like ambushes. Trust me, the struggle is real.

I've wrestled with my own so-called delightful demons—the relentless tug of perfectionism, chasing an ideal that likely doesn't exist. Add to that a full-blown case of Superwoman Syndrome, questioning my purpose, and wondering if all those years spent earning my doctorate really mattered. And then there's the uphill climb of deeper communication: finding both the courage and the grace to truly connect not only with the people around me, but with God Himself, in a way that feels authentic and unhindered.

Here's the powerful truth: my father's example doesn't just highlight these struggles, it shines a spotlight on the way through them. My real breakthroughs came when I finally put his lessons to the test, engaging with those foundational truths for myself. As I've navigated my own wild ride, what he embodies has shifted from theory to essential survival tools. Applying divine principles to real, messy life situations? Revolutionary. I've learned firsthand that living out faith isn't just powerful, it's the surest way to build a life anchored in purpose, overflowing with meaning, and profoundly rich.

Your #BestSelfie Journey Starts Now

Let's be real for a second. Life at this stage? It's a mix of holy moments and hot messes. We're out here balancing big dreams with grocery lists, praying for peace while reheating our coffee for the third time, and trying to remember if self-care includes folding the laundry or pretending it doesn't exist.

That's where this devotional comes in. It's my love letter to legacy — the kind passed down through faith, wisdom, and the occasional side-eye from someone who's been there. The truths you'll read here come straight from my father's teachings, seasoned with my own real-life lessons and a dash of millennial honesty.

You'll see *Power Shot* sections throughout. Those are your little daily boosts — the "words with purpose" that remind you who you are and who you're becoming. Because spiritual growth isn't just about what you do; it's about how you talk to yourself and to God. Naming those powerful traits — like *audacity*, *fortitude*, or *serenity* — helps you live them. It's not just vocabulary; it's spiritual vocabulary with attitude.

Now let's talk about how we actually build these habits — because we've all tried the "new me starts Monday" approach, and let's be honest... by Wednesday, we're tired and looking for snacks.

Enter the Tiny Habits Framework, created by Stanford researcher Dr. BJ Fogg. His studies show that the key to real, lasting change isn't doing *more* — it's starting *smaller*. When a habit is simple to start, feels good to do, and fits naturally into your day, it sticks. In other words: transformation happens one small, joy-filled step at a time.

Science calls it behavior design. I call it grace in motion.

You don't need to overhaul your life overnight. Just start smaller. Whisper a prayer before you scroll. Take one deep, holy breath before you react. Write one line of gratitude before you crash into bed. These tiny choices build momentum, and over time, they rewire your heart and habits toward peace, purpose, and joy.

So together, we're going to do just that! We will practice *tiny habits of faith, tiny habits of words, tiny habits of action,* and *tiny habits of becoming.* Little shifts that lead to big transformations.

And yes, you'll also meet Paws, Rev's loyal sidekick, who's basically proof that God uses the smallest things — and the furriest friends — to remind us that joy and faith go hand in hand.

So grab your mug, take a deep breath, and let's do this together. Not perfectly. Just faithfully. One tiny habit at a time.

So why call it *Unfinished Business*?

Because, honey, that's exactly what we are — beautiful, chaotic, holy works in progress. Over 40? Same. Overwhelmed? Most days. But still becoming? Absolutely.

This isn't about getting it all together; it's about keeping it together long enough to let God do His thing. Life doesn't slow down. The laundry still piles up, the inbox still mocks you, and the people you love still somehow forget to replace the toilet paper roll. But in the middle of all that noise, there's something sacred happening. God's still shaping you. He's not finished, not frustrated, and definitely not giving up.

See, *Unfinished Business* isn't a to-do list — it's an invitation. It's a reminder that even your small steps count. The quiet prayers. The deep breaths. The tiny habits that feel too simple to matter but somehow keep your soul afloat. Those are the moments that change everything.

This devotional is for the person who's juggling purpose and pressure, who's trying to keep their peace while finding their people, who wants to love Jesus but also sometimes wants to throw their phone into the ocean. (Relatable, right?)

We're not chasing perfection here. We're learning to pause, laugh, surrender, and try again — with grace, grit, and a good cup of coffee or tea.

So, as you move through these tiny habits, pay attention to the shifts — how you start to breathe a little deeper, worry a little less, and trust a little more. That's what growth looks like in real life.

God's still writing your story, and spoiler alert: it's good.

I dare you to give Him the praise of expectation. Because even if you can't see the ending yet... It's already done.

Butterflies in my stomach.
Gratitude in my heart. Finally doing it.

Dr. Shan

The Daily Grind

PART 1

Before You Pour Your First Cup...

Welcome to The Daily Grind—where caffeine meets calling and grace meets grit.

This is where faith and real life collide — not the Sunday-morning-polished kind, but the weekday kind. The kind where you spill your coffee, misplace your peace, and still show up praying, "Lord, please don't let me lose it today."

These next ten days are about finding God in the middle of the mess — in your traffic jam, your inbox, your unfolded basket of laundry, your kitchen sink. Because faith isn't just for quiet mornings; it's for loud, unfiltered living. Every little act of belief, every small moment of obedience, every whispered "help me, Jesus" counts.

You don't need to overhaul your life overnight. You just need one tiny habit of faith at a time — one thought, one prayer, one decision that keeps you anchored when life's blender hits "high."

So, grab your mug, take a deep breath, and lean in. This is your daily refill — strong, intentional, and blessed with purpose. Let's grind with grace.

Big *Faith* Energy

Daily Bean 

"Jabez cried out to the God of Israel, 'Oh, that you would bless me and enlarge my territory! Let your hand be with me, and keep me from harm so that I will be free from pain.' And God granted his request." — **1 Chronicles 4:10 (NIV)**

Sip of the Day 

Alright, Habit 1 — we're really doing this #SelfieLife thing. And we're kicking it off with a foundational habit that changes everything: bold, dependent prayer.

Let's be honest — sometimes our prayers sound more like quick texts to God than actual conversations. "Hey God, it's me again, just checking in. Please fix this, bless that, thanks, love ya." Most of us don't struggle to pray — we struggle to *pause* long enough to actually believe what we're saying. We rush through our prayers as if they're items on a checklist rather than invitations to intimacy. But this habit? It starts with the first letter in SELFIE: S — Stopping.

Stopping to breathe.

Stopping to listen.

Stopping long enough to remember who is actually in control.

That's what Jabez did. He stopped chasing outcomes and simply asked for God's hand to guide the next move. His prayer wasn't timid; it was bold, detailed, and unapologetic. He didn't whisper blessings — he called them out.

His story begins in pain. Literally. His name means "he causes pain." Talk about a rough start. Most folks would've accepted that label, settled for survival, and played it safe. But not Jabez. He dared to ask God for more — not for fame, not for status, but for divine *expansion*. He wanted more space to serve, to grow, and to live on purpose. And he didn't just want bigger blessings; he wanted God's hand on everything he touched. Because he knew, without divine direction, success can turn into stress real quick.

This isn't just a feel-good Bible story; it's your first tiny habit.

When you pray, don't shrink your requests to fit your comfort zone. Stretch your faith instead. Ask boldly — not because you're entitled, but because you trust God's generosity. Start your day by praying one specific prayer that makes you slightly nervous. Something that sounds too big for you but just right for Him.

Faith isn't polite; it's powerful. And sometimes your miracle starts with a prayer that makes Heaven pause and say, "Now that's faith I can work with." So go ahead, ask big. You're not inconveniencing God; you're inviting Him to move.

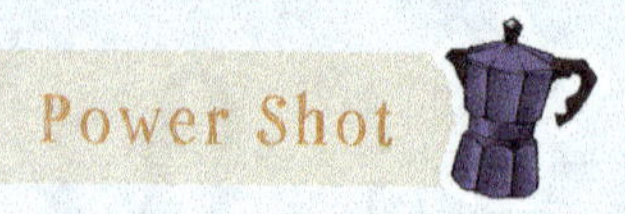

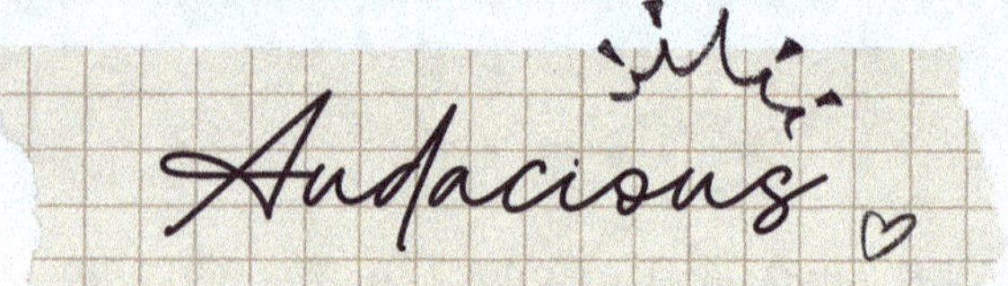

Audacious

Audacious:
(aw-DAY-shus) — adjective

Definition: Bold, daring, and willing to take surprisingly confident risks.

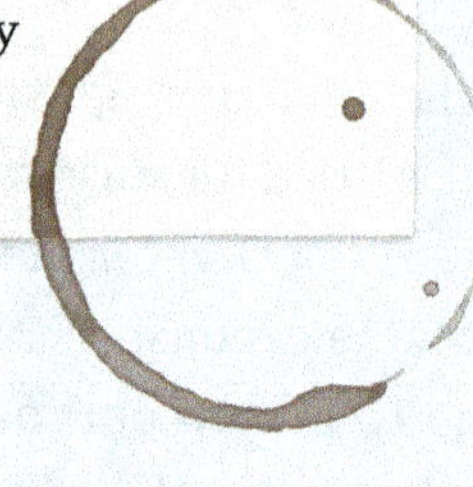

Rev Says 

"Too many of us pray with a teacup when God's got a mega-mug ready! Don't just complain about your small cup; have the **audacity** to ask God to fill a bigger one!"

God,
help me to pray with audacious faith. No more polite, half-hearted prayers. Please give me the courage to ask big, to trust deeply, and to believe boldly. Expand my territory and guide my steps. I'm ready to pray, knowing You can handle it. Amen.

- What's one area of your life where you've been praying small or safe?

____

____

____

____

____

- What bold, specific request can you bring to God today — something that stretches your faith?

____

____

____

____

____

Less Foam, More *flavor*

"For all those who exalt themselves will be humbled, and those who humble themselves will be exalted." — *Luke 14:11* (NIV)

"Humble yourselves, therefore, under God's mighty hand, that he may lift you up in due time." — *1 Peter 5:6* (NIV)

If Habit 1 was about praying big, today is about staying grounded while you rise. Because here's the truth — big prayers without humility? That's like a latte without espresso: looks good, but no real power. All foam. No flavor.

Let's clear something up: humility isn't about playing small or pretending you don't have gifts. It's not self-shrinking; it's soul-centering. True humility is your secret power move. It is the quiet strength that grounds you while God does the elevating. It's the realization that a Divine Maestro is running this show, and in case you have not realized, it's not you.

Humility isn't weak. It's wisdom. It's the courage to admit that you don't have to carry the universe (or your to-do list) on your shoulders. It's the freedom of knowing that you don't need to be the loudest voice in the room to make the biggest impact. Humility whispers what pride forgets: that grace flows downhill.

Here's your tiny habit for today:

Before you start your morning hustle, pause and say, "God, I surrender my need to control it all." Simple, right? But powerful. That one moment of surrender trains your heart to rely on God's strength, not your own — and that shift will change everything about how you show up.

Because humility doesn't hold you back — it sets you free. It protects you from pride when you succeed and lifts you when you stumble. It reminds you that every blessing, every win, every open door came by grace, not grind.

And Jesus? He doesn't play favorites. He pours out grace like confetti — His divine sparkle lands on hearts that stay humble. So, stand tall, stay teachable, and remember: humility isn't a posture of weakness. It's the foundation of strength that keeps your #BestSelfie anchored in God's favor.

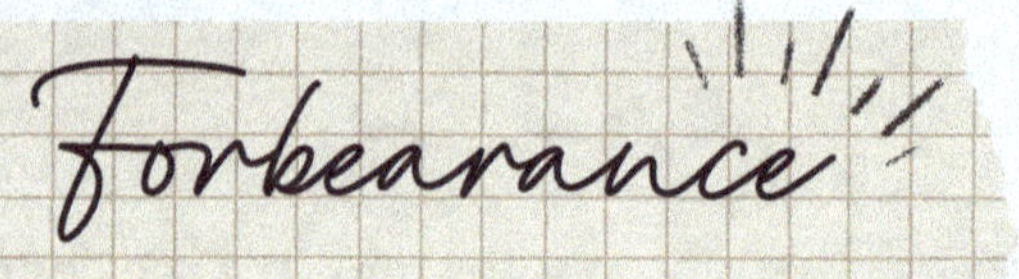

Forbearance

Forbearance:
(for-BEAR-uhns) — noun

Definition: Patient self-control; restraint; the ability to endure difficulty without complaint.

Rev Says 

"You ever bite your tongue when you could've said a whole lot more? That right there is **forbearance**. It's not easy, but it's powerful. Sometimes the strongest thing you can do is stay quiet, take a breath, and let God handle the heavy lifting. That kind of patience builds character faster than any spotlight ever could."

Lord,
teach me the beauty of forbearance. Help me stay patient and humble when I want to rush or react. Remind me that Your strength works best when I step back and let You lead. Keep me grounded, teachable, and full of quiet confidence in Your plan. Amen.

- When was the last time you caught yourself trying to control something only God could fix?

- How can you practice forbearance today in one small moment of frustration or pride?

Your *Faith* Formula

Daily Bean 

"Peace I leave with you; my peace I give you. I do not give to you as the world gives. Do not let your hearts be troubled and do not be afraid." — **John 14:27 (NIV)**

"But you will receive power when the Holy Spirit comes on you; and you will be my witnesses in Jerusalem, and in all Judea and Samaria, and to the ends of the earth." — **Acts 1:8 NIV**

"Know that the Lord is God. It is he who made us, and we are his; we are his people, the sheep of his pasture." — **Psalm 100:3 NIV**

Sip of the Day

Today we're unlocking what I like to call *the big life*: the one that says, "I woke up like this!" and helps you live as your brightest, most grounded self.

Ever feel like you're in a game of cosmic hide-and-seek with happiness? Always chasing that "just right" moment— a little more success, a little more peace, or finally feeling like you've made it? We're constantly flooded with formulas for flourishing, but God's design for abundance is refreshingly simple: seek Him first. When you do, everything else finds its proper place. It's like the universe exhales and whispers, "Finally, we're in alignment."

Here's your tiny habit for today:

Start your mornings by inviting God to guide your Four P's—Peace, Power, Pleasure, and Prosperity. Whisper this before you check your phone: "Lord, help me choose peace, walk in power, delight in You, and steward what You've given." It's simple, but it trains your heart to center on Him instead of the chaos around you.

Now let's peel back the layers. **Peace** isn't the zen kind you scroll for on Instagram; it's the deep calm that anchors you when the world spins out. **Power** isn't micromanaging yourself into exhaustion— it's the Holy Spirit's quiet courage that helps you face what's hard without losing your cool. **Pleasure** isn't fleeting indulgence or a little sweet treat—it's the joy of living in your God-given lane, knowing you're exactly where you belong. **Prosperity**? We love a good bank balance, but this is more than money. It's having enough time, love, strength, and resources to bless others.

Eudaimonia is the word for that kind of life: the flourishing, thriving, purpose-filled existence that comes when you let God lead. You don't chase it. You cultivate it. And it's also the "F" in your SELFIE habit: Finding Joy in What Is. Every time you pause to savor what's right in front of you, to see your peace as enough, your power as purpose, your pleasure as worship, and your prosperity as gratitude, you are practicing this habit. You are living your #BestSelfie Life — fully present, fully aligned, and flourishing from the inside out.

Eudaimonia

Eudaimonia:
(yoo-day-MOH-nee-uh) — noun

Definition: A state of flourishing, human thriving, and living well; a life of virtue in the pursuit of human excellence.

Rev Says

"Folks spend their whole lives chasing rainbows, thinking they'll find a pot of gold. But when you put God first, you get the rainbow, the pot, and maybe even the leprechaun thrown in! That's the secret to real **eudaimonia**—peace that lasts, joy that sticks, and blessings that don't quit."

Lord,
today I choose to seek You first.
Let Your peace settle my heart, fill me with the power of Your Spirit, restore my joy, and bless me with true prosperity that overflows into others. Help me live a life of eudaimonia—flourishing in Your purpose and resting in Your love. Amen.

- Which of the Four P's—Peace, Power, Pleasure, or Prosperity—do you most need God to strengthen in your life right now?

- How can you practice your tiny habit by seeking God first before you chase the next goal or distraction?

Ditching the Worry Weight

Daily Bean 

"Cast all your anxiety on him because he cares for you."
— *1 Peter 5:7 (NIV)*

Sip of the Day

Habit 4! Yesterday, we unpacked the Four P's that define a full, faith-first life. Today, we're tackling a heavy one: the habit that steals joy, drains peace, and sneaks into even the most put-together hearts—worry.

Let's be honest. Most of us wear anxiety like an accessory. We carry it to work, to bed, even to church, as if it's part of who we are. We convince ourselves that worrying means we care, that it keeps us prepared, that it somehow helps us stay in control. But worry is sneaky. It doesn't solve problems; it multiplies them. It's like carrying an invisible backpack stuffed with what-ifs, should-haves, and worst-case scenarios. It slows your stride and steals your sparkle.

Scripture gives us a clear, no-nonsense directive: *Cast all your anxiety on Him.* That isn't a gentle suggestion; it's a divine invitation to live lighter. Picture your mind like a high-performance engine—worry clogs the system, trapping you in loops of dread and overthinking until everything sputters.

Whenever you catch yourself spiraling in worry, say out loud, "God, I'm handing this to You." Do it as many times as you need. The act of releasing trains your mind to lean on God's care rather than your own fear. Each release is a faith rep, building spiritual muscle and replacing anxiety with trust.

And yes, sometimes worry feels deeper than a passing thought. Anxiety disorders, panic attacks, or perfectionism can make daily peace feel out of reach. That's when faith and wisdom work hand in hand. God, in His compassion, gave us counselors, doctors, and therapists who help untangle what our prayers reveal. Seeking that help isn't weakness—it's stewardship of your mental and spiritual health.

So, here's the truth: you don't have to carry what God is willing to lift. Every time you choose release over rumination, trust over tension, you reclaim a piece of your peace. Hand Him your what-ifs and watch Him hand back freedom. Because the One who calms the storm can handle your inbox, your diagnosis, your heartbreak, and your to-do list. He cares for you— truly.

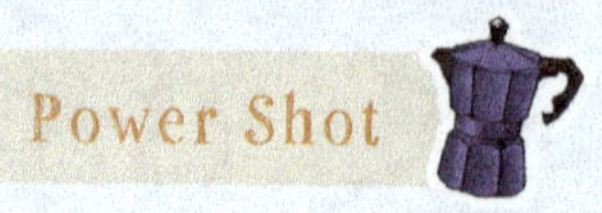

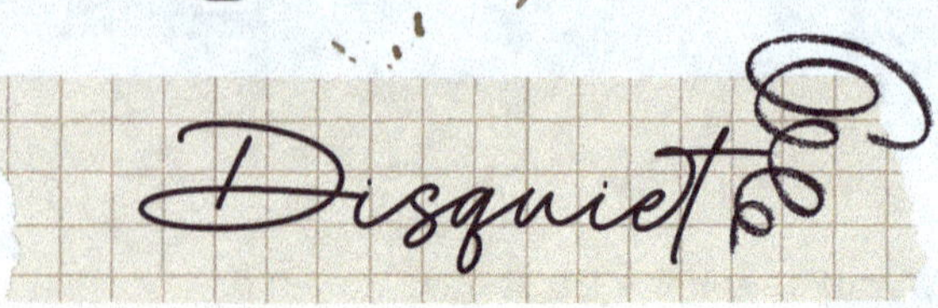

Disquiet

Disquiet:
(dis-KWAHY-it) — noun

Definition: A feeling of anxiety or worry; a state of uneasiness or agitation.

Rev Says

"Ever see a child let go of a balloon? Whoosh—gone! That's how you deal with **disquiet**. Let it go, and let God handle the wind. Holding on tangles you up, but releasing it makes space for joy to float in. God's arms are a lot bigger than your backpack of worries, so hand it over, sweetheart."

Lord,
I'm done carrying what You've already offered to hold. I cast my worries, fears, and anxious thoughts into Your care. When disquiet creeps in, remind me that peace is always available in You. Teach me to release what I can't control and rest in the truth that You care for me completely. Amen.

- What's been stealing your peace and stirring disquiet in your heart lately?

- How might your mood or mindset shift if you practiced releasing those worries as they show up?

Surfing the Storm

"When you pass through the waters, I will be with you; and when you pass through the rivers, they will not sweep over you. When you walk through the fire, you will not be burned; the flames will not set you ablaze." — *Isaiah 43:2 (NIV)*

You've dropped the worry weight, and now it's time to tackle the next test: the moments when life doesn't just drizzle—it floods. You know the kind. Those times when everything that could go wrong does, and you're left whispering, *"God, where are you in this?"*

Picture the Israelites standing at the edge of the Red Sea. Behind them, Pharaoh's army. Before them, a wall of water. No exit, no plan B, just panic. You can almost hear their collective sigh: *"Seriously, God? Now you disappear?"*

If you've ever stood in that space between fear and faith, you're in good company. We all hit moments that shake us—the job that vanished, the relationship that broke, the diagnosis that knocked the wind out of you. When everything collapses and your blueprint burns, trusting an invisible God with an invisible plan can feel impossible. But this story reminds us that faith isn't about your plan; it's about His presence.

Here's your tiny habit for today:

When things start spiraling, instead of rushing to fix it, panicking, or overthinking, pause. Here's where your SELFIE habit kicks in. The "S" reminds you to Stop. Literally stop, take one deep breath, and say, "God, I trust You in this mess." That single pause is sacred space. It's where panic ends and peace begins.

The Israelites didn't know the sea would part, but God did. He didn't need their strategy—He needed their stillness. Moses told them, "Do not be afraid. Stand still, and see the salvation of the Lord." That same promise still stands for you. God is not surprised by your Red Sea moments. He's not pacing Heaven, scrambling for solutions. He's steady, intentional, and fully capable of making a way where there seems to be none.

This week, let go of the urge to control the outcome. Instead, breathe, pray, and watch for the quiet miracles that rise out of chaos. The waters may roar, but they won't sweep you away. He's got you—and He won't let go.

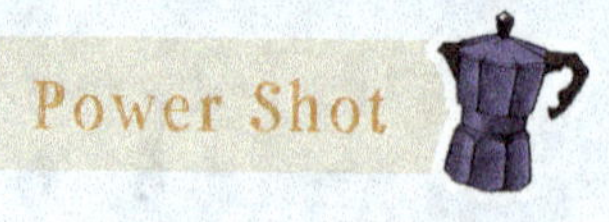

Consternation

Consternation:
(kon-ster-NAY-shun) — noun

Definition: Feelings of tension or dismay, often caused by something unexpected.

"Now listen, sometimes life's like standing at the edge of the Red Sea with your shoes on backward. You panic, you holler, and you start looking for the nearest raft. But that's when you must do what Moses said—stand still! God's the best Red Sea splitter there is. Hand Him your **consternation**, and He'll trade it for calm quicker than you can say 'hallelujah.'"

God, when my heart fills with consternation, remind me that You are not shaken by what scares me. Teach me to stand still and trust Your plan when I can't see the way forward. You fought for Moses, and you'll fight for me, too. I place every rising wave in Your hands and rest in the peace only You can give. Amen.

- What current "Red Sea" moment in your life is stirring up consternation or fear?

- How can you practice stillness and trust this week instead of trying to fix everything yourself?

Hands Off, Heaven's On

Daily Bean 

"The Lord will fight for you; you need only to be still."
— *Exodus 14:14 (NIV)*

Sip of the Day

Life can feel like a nonstop wrestling match some days, can't it? You're dodging deadlines, sparring with stress, and trying to keep your peace while the world throws punches. But Habit 6 brings a truth that changes everything: you don't have to fight every battle. Some fights belong entirely to God.

Think about it— how many times have you worn yourself out trying to fix, defend, explain, or control something that only Heaven could handle? You lose sleep, rehearse conversations, scroll for answers, and still end up exhausted. Meanwhile, God is whispering the same words He spoke to Moses: *"The Lord will fight for you; you need only to be still."*

Being still isn't passive. It's powerful. It's not giving up— it's giving over. The stillness God calls for is active faith in motion. It's the deep breath before the breakthrough, the pause that says, "I don't need to have the last word. God's already speaking on my behalf."

Habit 06

Vanquish the first negative thought that rises and invite God into the moment. The "E" in SELFIE reminds us to erase the negativity. This isn't denial — it's discipline. It's catching yourself mid-spiral and saying, "Nope, I'm not letting this live rent-free in my mind today." Every time you choose release over reaction, you make space for peace to do its work.

You're not weak when you step back; you're wise. You're choosing divine strategy over emotional impulse. God's not asking you to perform, persuade, or prove yourself—He's asking you to rest while He moves mountains.

So let Him. Whatever you've been wrestling with—fear, finances, family drama—hand it over. The God who split seas and silenced storms hasn't lost a fight yet, and He's not about to start now.

 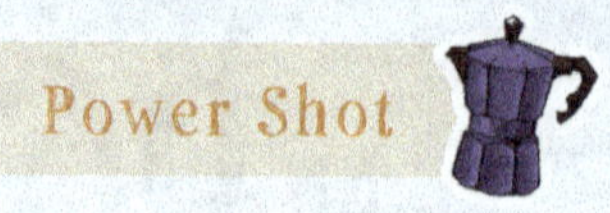

Vanquish:
(VAN-kwish) — verb

Definition: To defeat thoroughly;
to overcome completely.

Rev Says 

"Well now, I know you think you've gotta roll up your sleeves and handle everything yourself, but listen here: sometimes the smartest thing you can do is step aside. God's already out there fighting for you, ready to **vanquish** every mess trying to steal your peace. So quit shadowboxing with your problems—let the real Champion take the ring."

Lord,
thank You for being my Defender.
Today, I hand over the battles I've been trying to fight alone.
Teach me to be still when I want to strive, and to rest in Your
promise to vanquish every obstacle in Your perfect way. Help
me to trust Your timing, Your strength, and Your victory. Amen.

- What battle are you trying to fight with your own strength instead of handing it over to God?

- How can you practice stillness today, letting God vanquish what's been wearing you out?

Thankful *Trust*

Daily Bean 

"Rejoice always, pray continually, give thanks in all circumstances; for this is God's will for you in Christ Jesus."
— *1 Thessalonians 5:16-18 (NIV)*

Sip of the Day 

Alright, Habit 7! Yesterday, we learned how to let God fight the battles that keep us pacing the floor. Today, we're taking that trust and putting some gratitude on it. I call this *thankful trust*—and it's a total game-changer.

Let's not pretend we don't know that saying "Thank You" when life feels like a slow-motion train wreck isn't exactly easy. Gratitude doesn't come naturally when the bills are stacked, the inbox is overflowing, or the people you love are testing every ounce of your sanctified patience. But this habit isn't about pretending everything's fine; it's about remembering that God still is.

Scripture doesn't say "give thanks after it's all figured out." It says "in all circumstances." That's not spiritual denial—it's spiritual discipline. Thankful trust is the decision to praise before the payoff. It's the radical act of saying, *"God, I don't see the whole picture, but I trust the Artist."*

Here's your tiny habit for today:

Every time you catch yourself grumbling, trade the complaint for one sentence of gratitude. Out loud. "Lord, thank You that I'm learning patience through this," or "Thank You that You're still providing, even if it's not in the way I expected." One sentence. One shift. Gratitude in motion.

Because thankfulness in the middle of chaos rewires your focus. It reminds your spirit that peace isn't postponed until life gets pretty—it's available right now. When you live from a place of gratitude, worry loses its grip, perspective gets clearer, and faith grows stronger.

So stop waiting for the all-clear. Start thanking God in the middle of your messy masterpiece. Gratitude is your declaration that He's working, even when you can't see the blueprint. That's the heartbeat of the #BestSelfie life: joy, prayer, and praise—all rolled into one holy habit.

Gratification

Gratification:
(grat-uh-fi-KAY-shun) — noun

Definition: The feeling of contentment or satisfaction that arises from gratitude and fulfillment.

Rev Says 

"Some folks wait for sunshine and fireworks to say 'Thank you,' chasing big-time **gratification**. But the real pros? They can spot a blessing in a drizzle. Thank God right in the middle of the mess— that's thankful trust, plain and simple."

Lord,
teach me the rhythm of gratitude.
Help me give thanks not just when life feels easy, but when it stretches me. I choose gratification in all circumstances, trusting that You're weaving good even through the chaos. Please fill me with peace that outlasts the storm and joy that refuses to quit. Amen.

- What messy or uncertain area of your life could use a dose of thankful trust today?

- What's one small way you can turn a complaint into gratitude?

Run Your *Grace*

Daily Bean 

"You need to persevere so that when you have done the will of God, you will receive what He has promised." — *Hebrews 10:36 (NIV)*

Sip of the Day 

Alright, Habit 8! We've locked in thankful trust—gratitude on purpose, even when life's pitching curveballs. Now it's time to lace up for the next power move: *endurance*. Not the pretty kind, either. I'm talking about that gritty, sweaty, "keep-going-anyway" energy when everything in you wants to throw in the towel.

Endurance is what separates "I started strong" from "I finished faithful." It's not flashy. It's not quick. It's quiet consistency—showing up, again and again, even when you're tired, over it, or halfway convinced God forgot your address. But here's the thing: He didn't. He's training your faith muscles for the long haul.

The writer of Hebrews said it plainly: *"You need to persevere."* Not because God's playing hard to get, but because He knows every step strengthens your spirit. Think about Paul—a man who took more hits than a vintage video game hero, and still kept going. Why? Because he knew something we forget: this walk with God isn't a sprint. It's a marathon on the narrow road, complete with potholes, detours, and the occasional uphill struggle. But the finish line? Worth every step.

Here's your tiny habit for today:

When you feel yourself reaching for "I can't," pause and say, "But God can." Then take one more step— make the call, send the email, pray again, show up anyway. That's how endurance is built: one small, stubborn act of faith at a time.

God's not asking for perfect form—He's after forward motion. So, if you're limping, crawl. If you're crawling, breathe. But don't you dare stop. He's already equipped you with everything you need to finish strong.

Keep running, Selfie Superstar. You're not behind—you're becoming.

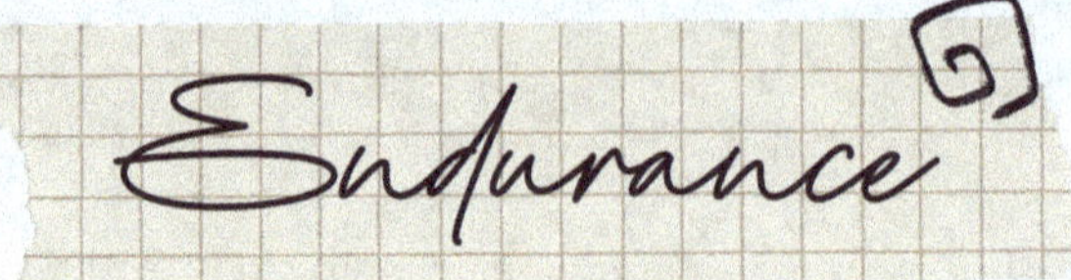

Endurance:
(en-DOOR-uhns) — noun

Definition: The ability to withstand hardship or adversity; the capacity to last or remain strong through challenge or wear.

"Life ain't no sprint, kid—it's an **endurance** game! You're going to hit some hills and potholes, maybe even trip over your own shoelaces. But the trick? Keep putting one foot—or paw, if you're Paws—in front of the other. God's got an energy refill waiting every time you think you're out of gas. Don't quit before the victory lap!"

Lord, thank You for setting a race before me. Some days I feel strong, other days I barely move, but You're steady through it all. Help me lay down every weight that's slowing me and run with endurance. When I'm weary, remind me that You're my strength and that my finish line is already marked with victory. Amen.

- What's one piece of "baggage" that's slowing your stride—fear, doubt, guilt—that you can let go of today?

- How can you take one tiny step forward this week, even if you don't feel like running?

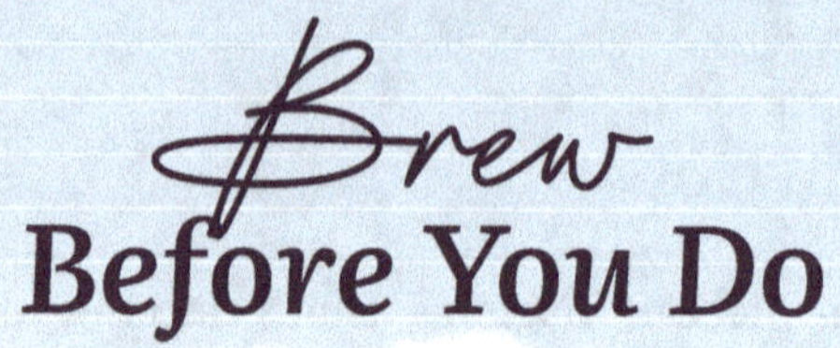

Brew Before You Do

Daily Bean 

"Commit to the Lord whatever you do, and He will establish your plans." — **Proverbs 16:3 (NIV)**

Sip of the Day

Habit 9, and we're talking about wisdom — not the kind that sounds deep on Instagram, but the kind that walks, talks, and shows up in your calendar and your choices. Because let's be real: half our stress isn't from what's happening — it's from what we *won't decide*.

Here's the truth: most "problems" aren't really problems. They are decisions dressed up in drama. We call it confusion, but often it's just hesitation in disguise. Proverbs 16:3 slices through the noise: *Commit to the Lord whatever you do, and He will establish your plans.* Translation? Stop spinning your wheels. Surrender the plan, trust the process, and watch God set the path.

And while we're at it, let's retire this line: "But I've never done this before." Philippians 1:6 already handled that one: *He who began a good work in you will carry it on to completion.* You're not underqualified, you're under-trusting. God doesn't need your résumé; He needs your *yes*.

Here's your tiny habit for today:

Before making any decision, pause long enough to *name your why out loud*. Ask yourself, "Is this wise, or just urgent?" Wisdom brings peace. Pressure brings panic. When your *why* aligns with God's will, you'll know — it'll feel steady, not strained.

That's how you live with wisdom in motion: not frantic, but focused; not perfect, but prayerful. The #BestSelfie life is built on that balance — spirit-led, not schedule-led.

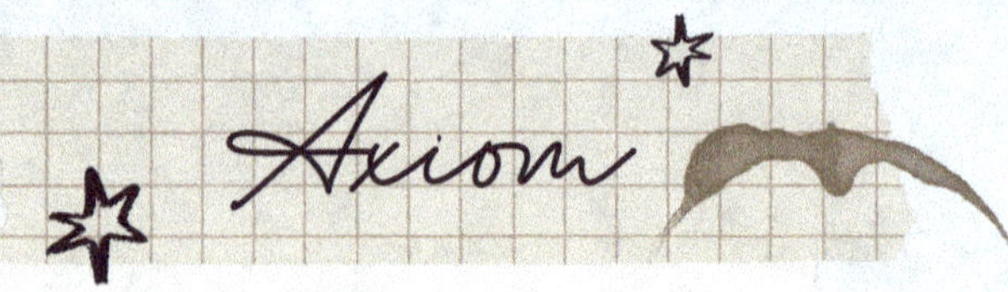

Axiom:
(AK-see-um) — noun

Definition: An established truth
or principle regarded as self-evident.

"Let me tell you something—the **axiom** of life is simple: think first, pray faster! Not every good idea's a God idea. Before you leap, check your why. If peace is pushing' you, move. If panic's driving' you, park it! God's wisdom doesn't rush."

Lord, thank You for the timeless axioms of Your Word. They are truths that never fail and wisdom that never expires. Teach me to pause and seek Your guidance before I commit, to test my why against Your will. Establish my plans, steady my spirit, and help me live out Your divine axioms in every decision I make. Amen.

- What "problem" in your life might actually be a decision waiting on wisdom?

- Where have you been rushing ahead instead of checking your *why* with God?

The *Launchpad* Principle

Daily Bean 

"And we know that in all things God works for the good of those who love Him, who have been called according to His purpose."
— **Romans 8:28 (NIV)**

Sip of the Day

Here we are…Habit 10. And today's truth? Sometimes your low point isn't punishment. It's preparation.

Okay, real talk: life has a way of knocking the wind out of you. You pray, you plan, you push forward — and then, boom. Something breaks. A dream detours. A door closes. You start wondering, *"Did I mess this up? Did God forget me?"* But friend, that's not the end of your story. It might just be the launchpad.

Think about Joseph. Betrayed, sold, falsely accused, thrown into prison — if anyone had a reason to give up, it was him. But here's the divine twist: every pit was part of the process. Without betrayal, there'd be no breakthrough. Without the prison, there'd be no promotion. Every painful moment was quietly paving the way for purpose. That's what Romans 8:28 means when it says God works *all things* together for good — not just the pretty parts, but the painful ones too.

When something goes wrong, say this out loud — *"This might be a launchpad."* Not "This is the worst," not "This is over." Just that simple statement of faith. Let it rewire your reflex. You'll start seeing disappointment as direction, not destruction.

Here's the real sip: faith doesn't mean you won't fall, it means the fall becomes a foundation. God is in the business of divine reversals. That closed door? It's redirecting you. That delay? It's refining you. That heartbreak? It's stretching your heart to hold something greater. You may feel buried, but maybe you've just been planted.

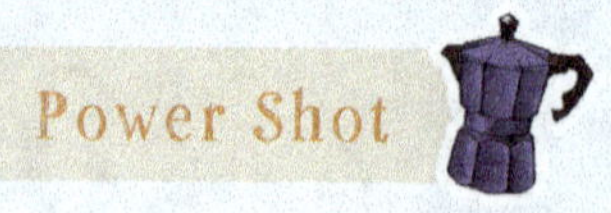

Catalyst:
(KAT-uh-list) — noun

Definition: A person or thing that
causes change or speeds transformation.

"Now listen here, kid — when life knocks you flat, don't panic. You're not stuck; you're stationed! That pit isn't permanent; it's a **catalyst**. God's just revving up His plans to launch you higher than you thought you could reach. So, chin up and trust the climb."

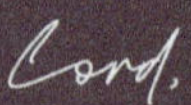

Lord,
thank You for being
the ultimate catalyst — the One who transforms my lowest
places into launching pads for Your purpose. When disappointment
hits, help me trust that it's not the end, but the beginning of something
new. Give me eyes to see Your design in my detours, and the faith to
believe that all things — yes, *all things*—are working for my good. Amen.

- Think about a low point you've been through or might be in right now. How could it be a *catalyst* for something new?

- What would change if you started to see every setback as part of God's setup?

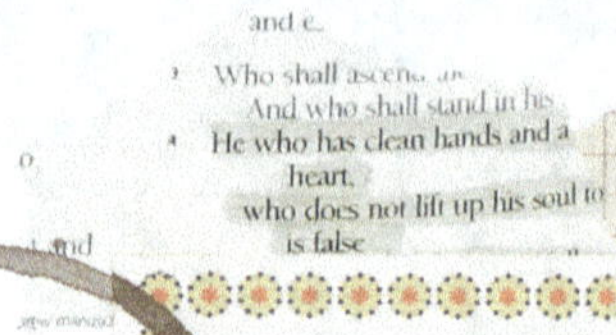

Pause & Pour

PART 2

If the Daily Grind is the hustle and The Next Stop is the vision, *Pause & Pour* is where we breathe. This is your divine coffee break — the space between doing and becoming. It's where your soul exhales and remembers that you don't have to sprint to stay in step with God.

You've been working hard on those habits, showing up, trying to grow, and maybe even wondering if it's working. But here's the secret every strong person of faith eventually learns: progress doesn't just happen in motion. Sometimes, the most powerful thing you can do is stop moving, stay still, and let God do the pouring.

This is where *Unfinished Business* hits a little deeper. You don't have to finish everything today — not the plan, not the project, not even the healing. God's not tapping His foot waiting on you to "get it together." He's patiently, tenderly completing what He started in you. And that, my friend, takes rest too.

So here's your reminder to practice your SELFIE habit — that sacred rhythm that keeps you grounded when life feels like too much:

S

STOPPING:

Hit pause. Put down the to-do list. Just stop running for a second.

E

ERASING THE NEGATIVITY:

Sweep out the mental junk.Fear, guilt, and the noise that says you're not enough.

L

LOOKING AROUND:

Notice the grace you missed while multitasking. God's been moving even when you didn't see it.

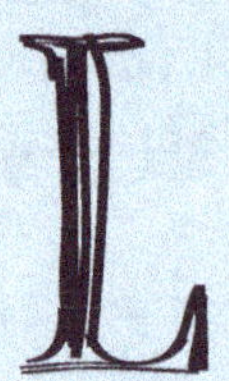

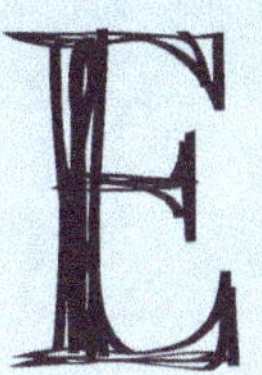

EXHALING:

Release the pressure to perform. Let go of the illusion that it's all on you.

INHALING:

Breathe in peace, purpose, and possibility. Let it settle into your spirit.

FINDING JOY IN WHAT IS:

Don't wait for perfect. There's beauty in the messy middle, too.

This isn't about losing momentum — it's about learning maintenance. You can't pour from an empty soul, and you were never meant to. So pause on purpose. Pour out the worry, and let God refill you with something better: perspective, patience, and peace for your next step.

You're not behind. You're not broken. You're becoming — and that's the real work of *Unfinished Business*.

Now breathe. Sip. Let's pause — and let Him pour.

Reflect Like a *Boss*

Daily Bean 

"Reflect on what I am saying, for the Lord will give you insight into all of this." — *2 Timothy 2:7 (NIV)*

Sip of the Day 

Alright, Habit 11, it's time to slow your scroll and check that spiritual mirror. Reflection isn't about replaying regrets; it's about realignment. This is your reminder to pause long enough to see what God's been doing *while* you were too busy doing everything else.

We're so good at analyzing everyone else's lives that we forget to sit with our own. Reflection is how you catch what God's been whispering all along — those little "aha" moments hidden inside ordinary days. Think of it like checking your rearview mirror, not to live in reverse, but to recognize how far you've already come.

Here's the secret sauce: reflecting like a boss isn't about marinating in the mess; it's about mining the meaning. Don't get stuck replaying old pain like a sad playlist. Instead, reframe it: *What did it teach me? How did it stretch me? Where did I see God show up when I almost gave up?*

Here's your tiny habit for today:

Set a timer for five minutes — yes, just five. Get quiet. Write down one verse or blessing that's been circling your mind. Don't overthink it; just sit with it. Let it sink in until gratitude starts to bubble up. That's reflection with intention.

Need some verses to ruminate on? Try these:

Philippians 4:6-7 (NIV): "Do not be anxious about anything, but in every situation, by prayer and petition, with thanksgiving, present your requests to God. And the peace of God, which transcends all understanding, will guard your hearts and your minds in Christ Jesus." (A potent reminder when worry weighs heavily.)

Psalm 23:1 (NIV): "The Lord is my shepherd; I lack nothing." (A simple yet profound picture of God's provision.)

Isaiah 41:10 (NIV): "So do not fear, for I am with you; do not be dismayed, for I am your God. I will strengthen you and help you; I will uphold you with my righteous right hand." (Perfect for those moments when the waters feel like they're rising.)

Reflection isn't a luxury; it's maintenance for your soul. When you take time to ruminate, your spirit gets sharper, your steps get surer, and your peace stops depending on what's happening around you.

Ruminate

Ruminate:
(ROO-muh-nayt) verb

Definition: To think deeply and at length; to ponder or meditate on something for an extended period, often thoughtfully and appreciatively.

Rev Says 

"You can't treat God's blessings like a snack bar. We're talking about a Sunday dinner for your soul—the good stuff! Think homemade macaroni and cheese and candied sweet potatoes. Don't just gobble it down; sit, savor, and truly **ruminate** on His amazing favor."

Lord,
help me to truly **ruminate** on Your goodness and my blessings today. Grant me the discipline to quiet my mind. As I reflect, give me fresh insight and wisdom for living, guiding me closer to Your perfect plan for my #BestSelfie Life. Amen.

- What verse, moment, or blessing do you need to ruminate on today?

- What insight has reflection given you about where God's been working behind the scenes?

Powered by *Purpose*

Daily Bean 

"Just as the Son of Man did not come to be served, but to serve, and to give his life as a ransom for many." — *Matthew 20:28 (NIV)*

Sip of the Day 

Alright, let's talk purpose — that big, beautiful word that both excites us and stresses us out. Everyone's talking about "finding their purpose," like it's a lost set of keys. But here's the truth: purpose isn't hiding from you. It's been in you all along, waiting for you to stop overcomplicating it.

Yesterday, we hit pause and reflected. That quiet moment you took? It wasn't wasted. It was preparation. Because purpose doesn't show up in chaos — it whispers in clarity.

Jesus modeled this perfectly. He didn't come flexing influence or status; He came to serve. That's the blueprint. Real power isn't loud — it's rooted in love, service, and divine direction. The world tells you to build a platform. God wants us to build people.

Serve with intention. Look for one person to help, encourage, or uplift — no announcement, no audience, no "look at me" moment. Just serve quietly and watch how that small act starts to shift something inside you. That's purpose-driven power — it flows *through* you, not *from* you.

And let's clear this up: living with purpose doesn't require a perfect plan or a glossy five-year vision board. God already drafted the blueprint. Your job is to stay available, not anxious. To say yes, even when you're nervous. To believe that your ordinary obedience can have an extraordinary impact.

You were created on purpose, for purpose. Your calling isn't a competition; it's a contribution. So today, trade the pressure to perform for the privilege of partnering with God. When you show up as His hands and feet, even the small stuff — a kind word, a patient moment, a prayer for someone who doesn't even know it — becomes Kingdom work.

So go ahead, be the light, not the spotlight. That's *Purpose-Driven Power.*

Vocation

Vocation:
(voh-KAY-shun) — noun

Definition: A strong sense of calling or suitability for a particular role or purpose —a divine assignment where your gifts meet God's timing.

Rev Says

"See that path, friend? That's your **vocation**! It's not about what you cooked up; it's about what God's got simmerin' for you. You're God's person, in God's perfect place, and He's got big plans to use you — one small act of love at a time. Don't just stand there, go be His hands and feet!"

Lord,
thank You for the privilege of purpose.
Teach me to walk in my vocation with humility and joy.
Help me remember it's *not I, but Christ* working through me.
Open my eyes to opportunities to serve, love, and reflect You
in the small moments that matter most. Amen.

- How does seeing your daily actions as part of your vocation — God's calling — change how you approach your work, family, or relationships today?

- What's one quiet act of service you can do this week that lets God's purpose shine through you?

Forward *Focus*

Daily Bean 

"Brothers and sisters, I do not consider myself yet to have taken hold of it. But one thing I do: Forgetting what is behind and straining toward what is ahead, I press on toward the goal to win the prize for which God has called me heavenward in Christ Jesus."
— **Philippians 3:13-14 (NIV)**

Sip of the Day

Letting go sounds easy until it is your turn to do it. Yesterday, we talked about purpose and living as God's hands and feet. Today, we are learning how to move those feet forward.

If you have ever tried running while dragging a suitcase, you already know the struggle. Carrying yesterday's weight slows you down before you even start. Paul said it clearly: forget what is behind. Forgetting is not pretending it never happened. It is choosing release over replay and growth over guilt.

You know that mental reel that starts with "If only..." or "I should have..."? It is time to silence it. You cannot run your #BestSelfie race while staring in the rearview mirror. Faith only moves in one direction, and that direction is forward.

Practice The Two-Step Reset. When you get out of bed, plant your feet, take two small steps forward, and say aloud, "Forward, God." Those two steps are your declaration that you are done looking back. Every morning becomes a physical reminder that grace always leads you onward.

God is not asking you to erase your past. He is inviting you to outgrow it. Every disappointment, delay, and detour has a lesson tucked inside it. Learn what you need to learn and keep walking. You are not who you were; you are becoming who He called you to be.

Lift your chin. Steady your stride. Step forward with peace and purpose. That is the direction of destiny.

Hinder

Hinder:
(HIN-der) verb

Definition: To create difficulties for (someone or something), resulting in delay or obstruction.

"See this anchor? That's what holding onto the past does– it just **hinders** your run towards your prize! Paul knew the secret: you gotta cut ties with yesterday's baggage to press on to what'snext. Drop that weight! The best view is always forward!"

Lord,
thank You that I do not have to live chained to what is behind me. Help me to release every weight that **hinders** and to keep my eyes fixed on what lies ahead. Teach me to walk with purpose and steady faith. Forward is where You are calling me. Amen.

- What anchor—regret, failure, or disappointment—might be hindering your forward motion?

- How can you make *The Two-Step Reset* part of your daily rhythm this week?

Cultivating Character

Daily Bean 

"But the fruit of the Spirit is love, joy, peace, forbearance, kindness, goodness, faithfulness, gentleness, and self-control. Against such things there is no law." — **Galatians 5:22-23 (NIV)**

Sip of the Day

We've moved forward; now it's time to grow deeper. Yesterday, we learned how to let go of what's behind us. Today, we're talking about something that decides how strong your future will be—character.

Character is the quiet proof of what God is doing inside you. It shows up when nobody's watching. It's how you respond when life gets complicated, inconvenient, or just plain irritating. It's who you are when the filters fall away and faith has to do the talking.

The "fruit of the Spirit" isn't a church buzzword or a checklist for perfect Christians. It's a lifestyle. Every time you choose grace when you could have snapped, or peace when you could have panicked, you're showing evidence that God's Spirit is alive and well in you.

The Fruit Focus. Each morning, pick one fruit of the Spirit to intentionally grow that day. Write it somewhere visible, whisper it in prayer, or set it as your phone reminder. When the day tests you (and it will), pause and ask, "How can I show this fruit right now?" That one question will turn challenging moments into training sessions for your soul.

God uses the ordinary to shape the extraordinary. The challenging coworker, the long line, the unexpected "why me" moments are not punishments; they're opportunities. Each one stretches you toward the person you're becoming.

The more you practice spiritual awareness, the more natural it feels. One day you'll catch yourself responding with peace instead of pressure, kindness instead of chaos, and realize— you've been growing all along.

Keep tending to the garden of your heart. The harvest takes time, but when it comes, everyone around you will taste the difference.

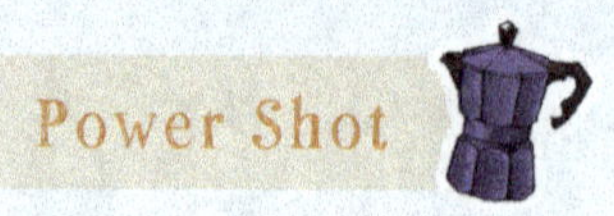

Cultivate:
(KUL-tuh-veyt) verb

Definition: To try to acquire or develop a quality, sentiment, or skill; to prepare and nurture growth.

"Ever tried keeping a houseplant alive? That's your character right there! You can't just plop it on a windowsill and forget about it. Every time you pick patience over pettiness, you're **cultivating** your character. Keep it up, or trust me—it'll wilt faster than week-old lettuce!"

Lord,

thank You for shaping me in both quiet and chaotic moments. Help me to **cultivate** the fruit of the Spirit, especially [Name the chosen fruit for the week]. Give me wisdom to respond with grace and strength to grow through every test. Amen.

- Which fruit of the Spirit (love, joy, peace, patience, kindness, goodness, faithfulness, gentleness, and self-control) do you want to focus on this week?

- What's one situation that could help you practice it in real time?

Slay Mode

Daily Bean 

"But thanks be to God! He gives us victory through our Lord Jesus Christ." — 1 Corinthians 15:57 (NIV)

Sip of the Day

Cue the theme music, because today we are stepping into *Slay Mode*. Yesterday, we talked about cultivating character, the daily work that builds your inner strength. Now it is time to walk in the confidence that comes from knowing who walks with you.

We all face giants. They show up as challenges, people, or situations that seem too big to handle. They talk loudly, steal peace, and test every ounce of faith you have. You try to pray them away, plan around them, or power through, and they just stare back like, "Still here."

Here is the truth that shifts everything. The battle is already won. When Jesus rose, He did not just win for Himself; He secured the victory for you, too. You are not fighting to win; you are standing in a victory that already belongs to you.

So when life starts shouting at you, whisper this truth: What He slays, I slay. When fear tells you that you are not enough, remind yourself that you are more than a conqueror. Slay! When discouragement creeps in, remember that victory is your birthright as a child of God. Slay!

One Minute of Motion. Each morning, before you scroll, sigh, or start, take one intentional minute to move and pray. Walk across the room, stretch, or sway to your favorite worship song—anything that gets your body awake and your spirit in sync with God.

As you move, speak gratitude and declare victory out loud.

"Thank You for what You have already done."
"Thank You that You are still working in my favor."
"Thank You that victory is mine in You."

It is not a workout; it is worship in motion. That single minute tells your mind, body, and soul, "We move with God today." By the time you stop, your energy has shifted, your focus has sharpened, and your spirit remembers the truth: you have already won.

Jesus can be your substitute for anything, but nothing can substitute for Him. When He is your source and your starting point, giants lose their power, and peace becomes your armor. You were not created to crumble under pressure. You were designed to conquer with purpose. So, lift your head, straighten your shoulders, and slay like the victory is already yours. Because with Him, it is.

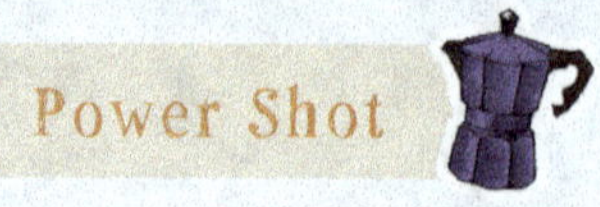

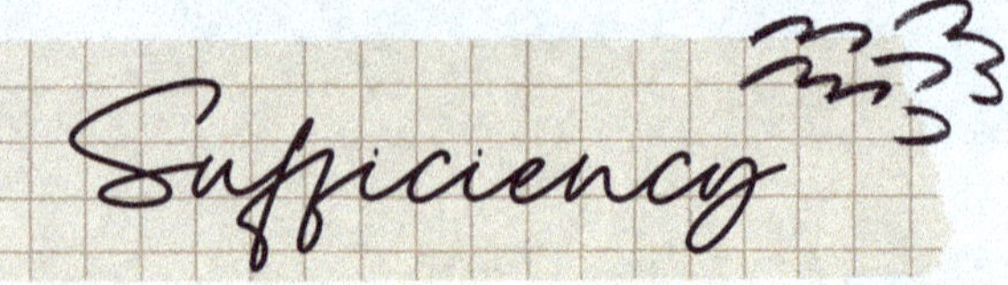

Sufficiency

Sufficiency:
(suh-FISH-uhn-see) noun

Definition: The quality of being adequate or sufficient; enough for a particular purpose; the state of being capable or competent.

"God is your **sufficiency** for every challenge, every struggle, every headache life throws at you. So tip your hat to Him, thank Him for the victory, and walk around like the conqueror you were made to be!"

Lord,
I declare Your **sufficiency** over every challenge in my life today. Because You are enough, I am enough. Amen.

- What "giant" or challenge in your life keeps trying to steal your peace?

- How can you practice the One Minute of Motion habit this week to remind yourself of God's sufficiency?

Confidence on Full Blast

Daily Bean 

"'Unless you people see signs and wonders,' Jesus told him, 'you will never believe.' The royal official said, 'Sir, come down before my child dies.' 'Go,' Jesus replied, 'your son will live.' The man took Jesus at his word and departed." — **John 4:48-50 (NIV)**

Sip of the Day 

You have already been walking in victory, and today it is time to level up. Habit 15 reminded you that what Jesus slays, you slay. Habit 18 calls you to believe that it is already done. This is faith on full blast.

In John 4, a royal official comes to Jesus, desperate for help. His son is dying, and he is out of options. He begs Jesus to come heal him in person, but Jesus only says, "Go. Your son will live." There is no touch, no scene, no proof — just a word.

And here is the powerful part: "The man took Jesus at his word and departed." That is the definition of faith. No confirmation email. No tracking number on the miracle. Just trust.

This is where confident faith begins. It is not about pretending the situation looks good; it is about knowing that God is good no matter how the situation seems. When Jesus speaks, results follow. So stop waiting for the perfect sign. Start walking in His promise.

Here is your tiny habit for today:

The One-Line Affirmation. Each morning, before you pick up your phone, say this out loud:

"I take God at His word today."

Say it until your spirit believes it. Whisper it when worry starts creeping in. Write it where you will see it often. The goal is not hype; it is holy confidence.

Faith like this changes everything. It strengthens your stance, silences your doubt, and shifts your atmosphere. You do not have to see the evidence to know the outcome. If Jesus said it, you can walk like it is already handled.

You are not walking by sight anymore. You are walking with certainty, moving through every moment with confidence on full blast.

That's how you live your #BestSelfie life—fully trusting, fully alive, fully His.

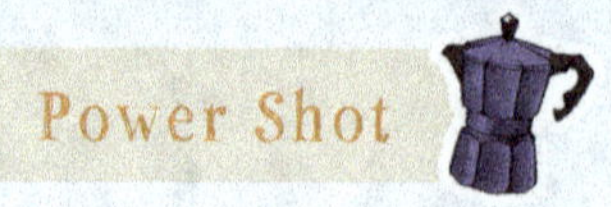

Assurance

Assurance:
(uh-SHUR-uhns) noun

Definition: A positive declaration intended to give confidence; a promise; confidence or certainty in one's own abilities or in the reliability of something.

"Unwavering **assurance** breaks down to this: When you trust Jesus, you don't need to see the whole picture. Just take Him at His word. He's got the power, and He won't let you down. That's a promise you can bank on!"

Lord, thank You for Your limitless power and Your unwavering **assurance**. I surrender my doubts, fears, pride, and guilt to You today. I choose to trust in Your saving word, Your love, and Your healing power. I have expectant faith that You will meet me where I am and bring the healing, pardon, change, and restoration I need for my #BestSelfie Life. Amen.

- Where do you need to show confident faith today, rather than waiting for proof?

- How can *The One-Line Affirmation* help you walk with assurance this week?

The *Active* Wait

Daily Bean 

"But if we hope for what we do not yet have, we wait for it patiently."
- **Romans 8:25 NIV**

"Wait on the Lord: be of good courage, and He shall strengthen your heart: wait I say, on the Lord." — **Psalms 27:14 (NIV)**

Sip of the Day 

By now, you've prayed bold prayers, practiced humility, shown gratitude, trusted through fear, and built spiritual muscle through sixteen powerful habits. You've stayed consistent, hopeful, and obedient. And yet... the breakthrough hasn't come — at least not the way you expected.

Maybe you're waiting for a door to open, a call to come through, or a season to shift. You've journaled, cried, praised, and done *all the things*, and it still feels quiet. But friend, God's silence doesn't mean He's ghosted you. It means He's working in ways you can't yet see. The waiting room isn't punishment — it's preparation.

Romans 8:25 reminds us that real patience isn't passive. It's an active, faith-filled trust. It's the kind of waiting that keeps your spirit awake and your hands ready. You don't stop believing; you start preparing for what you prayed for.

Habit **17**

When life feels stalled, *set the table* anyway. Literally. Choose one small physical act that represents your faith that God's promise is still coming.

- Waiting for reconciliation? Write the letter you'll send when peace returns.

- Waiting for a job? Iron your interview outfit or update your résumé tonight.

- Waiting for healing? Plan the celebration meal for when you feel better.

- Waiting for purpose? Clear a workspace and label it "God's next idea."

Each time you do this, you're saying with your actions, "*I believe it's on the way.*" That's what active waiting looks like—faith that's dressed and ready for the miracle.

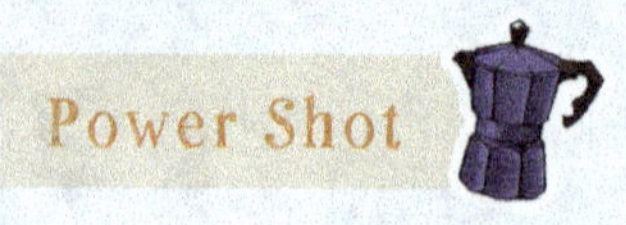

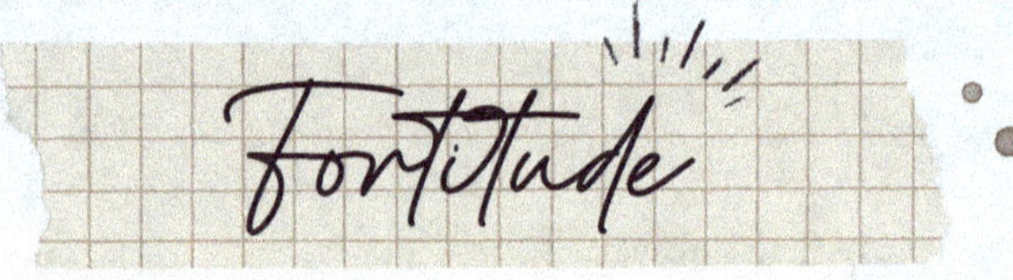

Fortitude

Fortitude:
(FOR-ti-tood) noun

Definition: Courage in pain or adversity; mental and emotional strength when facing difficulty, danger, or temptation.

Rev Says

"Now don't go sittin' there tapping your foot like you're in line at the DMV. God's building **fortitude**, not frustration! So, keep busy in belief. Set that table, wash that cup, act like company's coming, because it surely is."

Lord,

You see my heart.

I've prayed, hoped, and waited. Help me to wait well—with courage, faith, and **fortitude**. Let my actions show that I believe You're already working. Remind me that this pause is part of Your plan, and when You move, I'll be ready. Strengthen my heart as I wait on You for my #BestSelfie Life. Amen.

- What have you been faithfully waiting for that's starting to feel delayed?

- What specific action can you take today to set *the table* for that answered prayer?

Grace on Tap

Daily Bean 

"What Jesus did here in Cana of Galilee was the first of the signs through which he revealed his glory; and his disciples believed in him." — **John 2:11 (NIV)**

Sip of the Day 

Today we're talking about grace — the good stuff that keeps you glowing when everything else feels spent. You've been doing the work, forming tiny habits, and letting faith stretch you in ways you didn't even know were possible. Now, it's time to breathe in some joy.

In John 2, the wedding at Cana was buzzing with celebration until someone realized the wine was gone. The joy meter dropped, the hosts panicked, and everyone looked for a fix. Then Jesus stepped in. No grand entrance, no speeches. Just a quiet transformation that changed everything. Ordinary water became 150 gallons of the best wine anyone had ever tasted. That's how grace moves — not loud, but life-changing.

That's what grace does. It steps into the ordinary moments of your life and fills them with extraordinary joy. Grace meets you in the middle of your schedule, your stress, your uncertainty, and your weariness. It's God saying, "You don't have to do this on empty. I've got you covered."

So if your faith feels flat or your motivation is running low, it's time for a refill. Grace is on tap, ready and waiting for you. You don't have to earn it. You just have to receive it.

Here's your tiny habit:

The First Sip Reset. Tomorrow morning, when you pour your first cup of coffee, tea, or water, pause before you sip. Whisper, "Lord, refill me." Feel that warmth and let it remind you that grace is fresh every morning. No leftovers, no limits. Start your day with that mindset and let grace flavor everything that follows.

So if your faith feels or your motivation is running low, it's time for a refill. Grace is on tap, ready and waiting for you. You don't have to earn it. You just have to receive it.

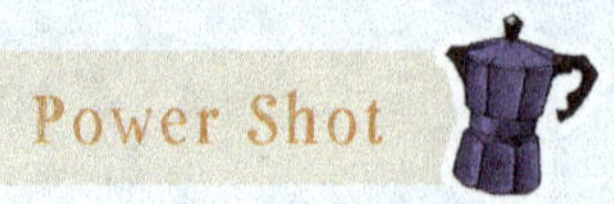

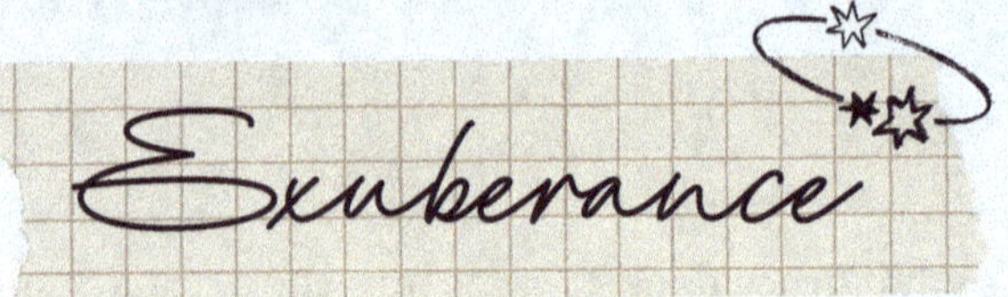

Exuberance:
(ig-ZOO-buh-ruhns) noun

Definition: The quality of being full of energy, excitement, and cheerfulness; a state of lively, enthusiastic joy.

"You ever seen a cup overflow, kid? That's how God pours grace. It doesn't stop at the rim. It keeps on goin'. Let Him fill you till you're spillin' joy all over the place. That's **exuberance** worth catching."

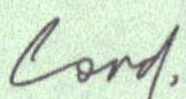

thank You for the grace that meets me in the middle of my ordinary. Fill me again until I overflow with peace, laughter, and exuberance. Help me carry that grace into every space I step into today. Amen.

- Which part of your life could use a refill of grace today?

- What's one everyday moment where you can slow down and actually taste that grace instead of rushing past it?

Watch Him *Work*

Daily Bean 

"Some time later, Jesus went up to Jerusalem for a Jewish festival. Near the Sheep Gate was a pool called Bethesda, with five covered colonnades. A large crowd of disabled people gathered there: the blind, the lame, the paralyzed. When Jesus saw him lying there and learned he had been in this condition a long time, he asked, 'Do you want to get well?

'Sir,' the man replied, 'I have no one to help me into the pool when the water is stirred. While I am trying to get in, someone else goes down ahead of me.' Then Jesus said, 'Get up! Pick up your mat and walk.'

At once, the man was cured; he picked up his mat and walked."
— **John 5:1-9, NIV (selected verses)**

Sip of the Day 

This is where faith gets practical. You've prayed, reflected, waited, journaled, trusted, and maybe even wondered if all that effort was doing anything. You've practiced every tiny habit so far, and you're wondering, "Okay, God, *when's my turn?*" If that's you, today's habit may hit home.

Picture the pool at Bethesda. Hundreds of people pressed around the water, waiting for that one moment when the surface rippled. The rule was cruel: only the first one in the pool got healed. Everyone else waited again. Day after day, the man Jesus saw lay there watching others get what he longed for. Thirty-eight years of disappointment. Thirty-eight years of "almost."

Then Jesus shows up, not as a spectator, but as the Savior who rewrites the rules. He doesn't tell the man to crawl faster. He doesn't lecture him for not trying harder. He asks, "Do you want to get well?" That question slices through excuses and self-pity like light through fog. Maybe that's what He's asking you today. Not because He doesn't know your situation, but because He wants your agreement. Healing isn't just about the body—it's about willingness, alignment, and faith that dares to stand up when everything still looks the same.

Here's your tiny habit:

Start keeping a Miracle Memo. Each evening, grab your phone or journal and jot down one place you saw God at work today. Title it "*Watch Him Work.*" It doesn't have to be dramatic— a problem that eased, a bit of peace in chaos, a laugh that came out of nowhere. Over time, you'll see a trail of small miracles that prove He's been moving all along.

Sometimes, your miracle doesn't splash in with fireworks; it unfolds quietly when you finally let go of how you thought it had to happen. Maybe God's already moving behind the scenes, shifting pieces you can't see. The invitation is simple: stop watchin**g the water and start watching Him work.**

Intervention

Intervention:
(in-ter-VEN-shun) noun

Definition: The action or process of intervening; an instance of interfering in any state of things or events to improve it or prevent it from getting worse.

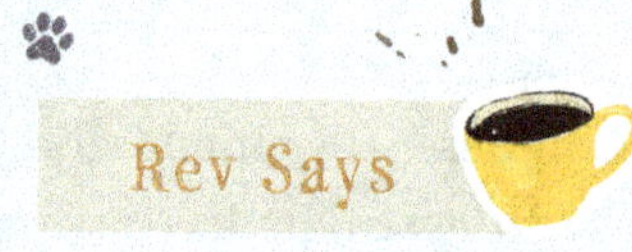

Rev Says

"Feeling helpless, like nothing's ever gonna change? That Bethesda story screams one thing: you don't need a magical puddle; you need a powerful Savior! Sometimes, God's divine **intervention** looks like Him walking right up to your impossibility and saying, 'Get up!' Don't wait for the water to stir; look for the one who stirs *life!*"

Lord,
thank You for stepping into my impossible places. When I feel stuck orforgotten, remind me that You are still moving. Help me to notice Your hand in every detail and to trust that Your intervention is already underway. I choose to rise in faith, watch You work, and walk boldly into my #BestSelfie Life. Amen.

- What situation in your life feels stuck, like you've been lying beside the same "pool" for far too long?

- Begin your Miracle Memo on the lines below to help you notice and celebrate God's quiet moves this week.

Never Running On Empty

Daily Bean 

"Some time after this, Jesus crossed to the far shore of the Sea of Galilee (that is, the Sea of Tiberias), and a great crowd of people followed him because they saw the signs he had performed by healing the sick. Then Jesus went up on a mountainside and sat down with his disciples... When Jesus looked up and saw a great crowd coming toward him, he asked Philip, 'Where shall we buy bread for these people to eat?' He asked this only to test him, for He had already decided what he was going to do. Philip answered him, 'It would take more than half a year's wages to buy enough bread for each one to have a bite!'"
— **John 6:1-5 NIV (selected verses)**

Sip of the Day 

We've seen God heal. Now we see Him provide — wildly, abundantly, and on a scale that silences doubt. Habit 20 is all about learning to trust that same extravagant power when life feels like you're running on empty.

Picture the scene: a massive crowd, hungry after following Jesus all day. The disciples, being practical folks (and a little stressed), just wanted to send everyone home. They quickly did the math and realized, "Uh, Lord, we don't even have enough cash to buy *a bite* for everyone here!" Sound familiar? Like us, they complained they didn't have the resources.

But Jesus, ever the master of the unexpected, didn't panic. He took the ridiculously small offering they *did* have – five loaves of bread and two fish, basically a kid's lunchbox – gave thanks to His Heavenly Father, and then started distributing. And distributed. And distributed. Until everyone — every one of the five thousand men, women, and children — was completely satisfied. Not just "not hungry anymore," but satisfied.

Here's your tiny habit:
The Open-Hand Challenge.

Whenever you feel anxious about not having enough time, money, ideas, or energy, pause and open your hands. Whisper, "*Lord, You are my source.*" That simple motion teaches your body what your spirit already knows: faith receives better than fear holds. Open hands make room for blessing.

The feeding of the 5,000, once again, dramatically shows God's remarkable munificence and His incredible kindness towards us. When God gives, He doesn't do it stingily; He gives abundantly! He gives more than we need for ourselves, so that we may have something to share with others. Do you truly trust that God will always provide for you as He has promised? And do you, in turn, share freely with others, especially those who lack? Today, ask God to fill you with gratitude and bless you with a generous heart, so you can freely share the incredible, limitless supply He pours into your #BestSelfie Life.

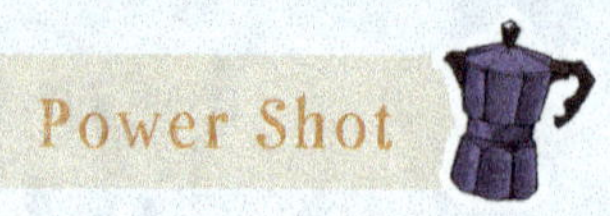

Munificence

Munificence:
(myoo-NIF-uh-sense) noun

Definition: The quality or action of being extremely generous; lavish generosity.

Rev Says

"You ever see a kid clutch a cookie so tight it crumbles? That's how we act sometimes with God's blessings. Loosen your grip and trust His **munificence**. He's got more waiting for you than you can hold."

Lord,

thank You for being munificent. Forgive me for gripping worry more tightly than Your promises. Today, I open my hands and heart to You. Fill me with confidence in Your provision, and teach me to live generously so my life reflects Your abundant grace. Amen.

- Where in your life are you holding on too tightly because you're afraid there isn't enough?

- How can you practice open-handed trust this week and let God's munificence flow through you?

The Next Stop: #BestSelfie Life

PART 3

Reflection. Renewal. Radiance.

Look at you. You've brewed bold prayers, poured out trust, and stirred up endurance. You've practiced the tiny habits that build your faith, word by word and step by step. You're standing in the glow of everything God's been growing in you. Welcome to The Next Stop — the part of your #BestSelfie journey where faith feels lighter, joy runs deeper, and your cup is finally full.

This is the stretch where you stop striving and start shining. You've done the heart work, and it shows. Rev's standing there in that golden light, mug raised high, not because the story's over — but because it's getting good. Paws is calm, the horizon's bright, and the air hums with peace.

This is **resplendence**. It's what happens when you walk with God long enough to realize that even the detours had purpose. You don't have to have it all figured out; you have to keep showing up with a full mug, an open heart, and a ready spirit.

So, here's to the next stop — where unfinished business turns into unstoppable faith. Keep your eyes on the horizon and your joy turned up. You've made it through the grind; now it's time to glow in the grace.

Your #BestSelfie Life starts right here.

Calm in the Chaos

Daily Bean 

"When evening came, his disciples went down to the lake, where they got into a boat and set off across the lake for Capernaum. It was already dark, and Jesus had not yet joined them. A strong wind was blowing, and the waters grew rough. When they had rowed about three or four miles, they saw Jesus walking on the lake and coming toward the boat. They were terrified. But he said to them, 'It is I; don't be afraid.' Then they were willing to take him into the boat, and immediately the boat reached the shore where they were heading." — **John 6:16-21 NIV (selected verses)**

Sip of the Day 

Yesterday, we marveled at God's generosity as we watched Him turn a small meal into a feast for thousands. Today, in Habit 21, we move from a full belly to a stormy sea—a reminder of where to find peace when life gets rough.

Picture it: Jesus says, "Get in the boat and head to the other side." Simple enough. They obey, but by nightfall, a windstorm rises. These are seasoned fishermen, yet even they panic as the waves pound. Sounds like an ordinary Tuesday, doesn't it? Then, out of nowhere, a figure walks across the water. Terror spikes until they hear the voice: "It is I. Don't be afraid." The moment He steps into the boat, the storm stops. No gradual fade-out, no cinematic sunset—just immediate calm.

They knew the water. They knew the waves. Yet exhaustion set in. That's where the over-40-and-over-it crew nods hard. We can juggle kids, work, bills, and expectations, but there comes a night when our arms give out. That's when grace shifts from concept to oxygen. Jesus doesn't shout from the shore; He steps on top of what's trying to sink you and comes close enough for you to see His face. That isn't motivation—it's presence.

Notice the sequence. The disciples are terrified. He names Himself: "It is I." Then peace arrives at the speed of surrender. The storm doesn't wind down with a pretty sunset; it stops because the One who made the wind tells it to hush. You don't need five backup plans. You need the right person in your boat.

Here's the tiny habit:

When the gusts pick up, don't grip harder—invite Jesus in sooner. Say it out loud if you have to: "Lord, get in this boat—this meeting, this budget, this mood." Calm isn't the absence of weather. Calm is the result of better company. Every time you choose presence over panic, you train your nervous system to recognize peace. You'll still row.

But your rhythm changes from frantic to faithful. And you'll look back later and realize you reached the shore faster than fear predicted.

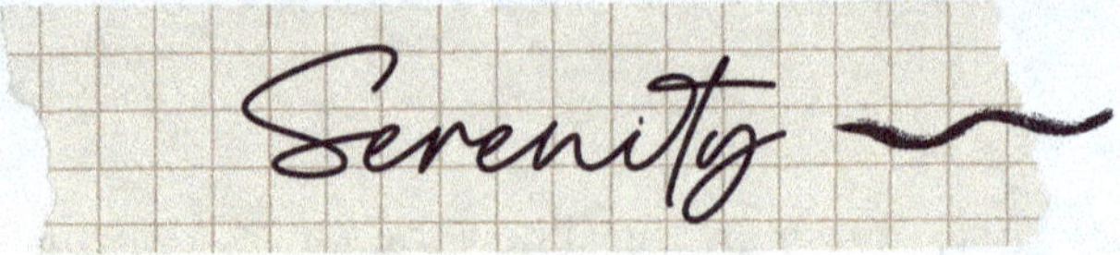

Serenity:
(suh-REN-i-tee) noun

Definition: The state of being calm, peaceful, and untroubled.

"Feeling like your boat's about to capsize? Winds howling, waves crashing? Been there! But remember, Jesus doesn't just *tell* the storm to stop; He *enters* your storm! That's when you find true **serenity.** So next time the waves hit, invite Him in. He's got your back, and your boat!"

Lord,
thank You for being the Master of wind and wave. I confess I try to navigate life's storms alone. I welcome You into my boat today. Speak peace over my fears and bring serenity to my chaos. I trust You to calm every storm in my #BestSelfie Life. Amen.

- What "windstorm" or "rough waters" are you facing that feel too heavy to handle alone?

- How can you intentionally invite Jesus into that situation today, trusting His presence to bring serenity?

The Mind Makeover

Daily Bean 

"Do not conform to the pattern of this world, but be transformed by the renewing of your mind. Then you will be able to test and approve what God's will is—his good, pleasing and perfect will."
— **Romans 12:2 (NIV)**

Sip of the Day

It's time to tackle the ultimate internal upgrade: a mind makeover. Ever feel like your brain is stuck on an old, glitchy operating system, constantly running outdated programs of worry, comparison, or negativity? Or catch yourself replaying thoughts that sound like "the world's greatest hits" album? Romans 12:2 calls us out on it in the best way possible!

Romans 12:2 doesn't say "try your best to think positively." It commands a transformation. God's telling us to stop letting the world set the pattern and let Him redesign our mental space from the inside out. The moment your mind starts to renew, your entire perspective shifts. You begin to see what God sees. You start recognizing what's truly "good, pleasing, and perfect."

The world trains us to hustle for validation, chase trends, and call stress a lifestyle. But Heaven runs on a different system. God says, "Uninstall the lies. Reboot your peace." It's not weird—it's wisdom. When you change how you think, everything else in your #BestSelfie Life starts aligning with His truth.

Here's your tiny habit:

Before you dive into your day, take one intentional minute for a *mental reset*. Whisper this prayer: "Lord, renew my mind right here, right now. Replace every anxious thought with Your peace and every negative word with Your truth."

That's it. One minute of rewiring your inner world before the outer world gets loud. Do it daily. Over time, you'll notice the shift—less reacting, more responding; less chaos, more clarity; less striving, more surrender. That's not wishful thinking. That's transformation!

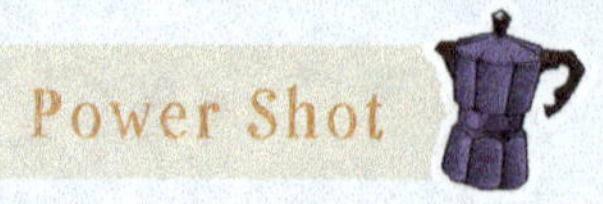

Metamorphosis

Metamorphosis:
(met-uh-MOR-fuh-sis) noun

Definition: A change of the form or nature of a thing or person into a completely different one, by natural or supernatural process; a transformation.

"Your mind's not a lost cause—it's a masterpiece under renovation! Let God swap out those old, toxic thought patterns with brand-new truth. That's the real **metamorphosis**: thinking higher, living freer, walking lighter. Now that's a makeover that sticks."

Lord,
my mind gets crowded with worries and distractions I didn't even invite in. Help me declutter my thoughts and make space for Your truth. Give me the courage to think differently—to think higher. Begin a metamorphosis in me that renews my focus, restores my peace, and keeps me walking in Your perfect will for my #BestSelfie Life. Amen.

- What old mindset has been holding you hostage—comparison, fear, perfectionism, or something else?

- How can you let God begin a metamorphosis in that area today?

The *Progression* Play

Daily Bean

"Now there were four men with leprosy at the entrance of the city gate. They said to each other, 'Why stay here until we die? If we say, "We'll go into the city," the famine is also there, and we will die. And if we stay here, we will die. So let's go to the Arameans' camp and surrender. If they spare us, we live; if they kill us, then we die.'"
— *2 Kings 7:3-4 (NIV)*

Sip of the Day 

Life is full of choices. Sometimes, though, it can feel like every option leads to a dead end.

In our scripture today, we meet four men with leprosy who are stuck outside a city gate during a famine. Talk about a tough spot! They faced three options, and at first glance, each seemed to lead to the same result: death.

If they stayed put, they'd starve.

If they went back, the famine would finish them off.

If they moved forward, the enemy might kill them.

Every option screamed *impossible*. Yet in the middle of all that hopeless logic, something brave sparked. The men with leprosy asked the question that changes everything, "Why stay here until we die?" That's the spirit! They realized that sitting still was just another way of giving up. And guess what? Their bold move opened the door to abundance not just for them, but for an entire city!

Sometimes faith looks less like fireworks and more like movement. One step. One decision. One "let's try." Progress often feels risky because it is—but staying stuck guarantees decay.

Here's your tiny habit:

When you feel trapped between bad options, choose forward anyway. Whisper this prayer: "Lord, meet me in motion." Then take one practical step—send the email, make the call, apply for the job, forgive the person, start the plan, go on the date. You'll be amazed at how God multiplies movement once you make it.

Your #BestSelfie Life isn't about perfect plans—it's about courageous progression. God can't steer what's parked. So start the engine.

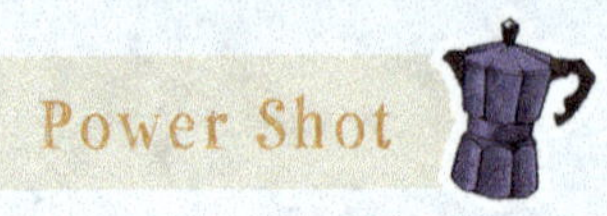

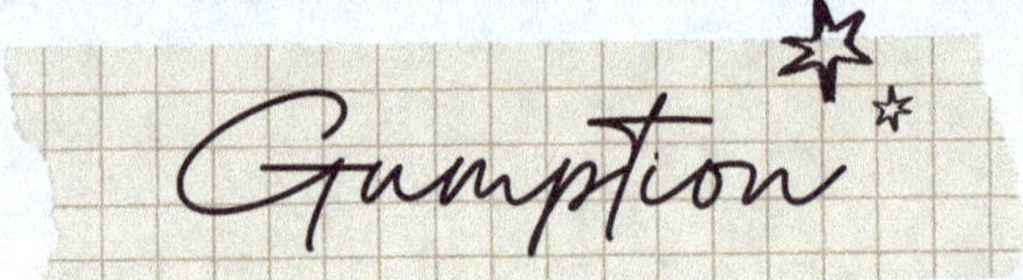

Gumption

Gumption:
(GUMP-shun) noun

Definition: Shrewdness and initiative; courage and common sense.

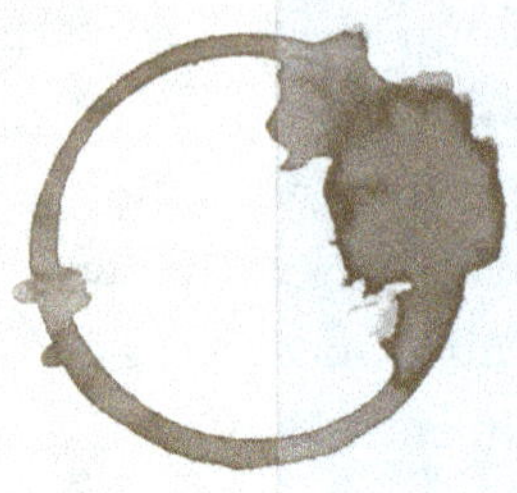

Rev Says

"Ever feel like those fellas at the gate, sittin' there thinking, 'Well, this is it'? Don't camp out in defeat! God gave you **gumption** for a reason. Sometimes all He needs is a little movement so He can meet you halfway. Take that first step—He'll handle the rest."

Hey God, when I feel stuck and scared to move, remind me of those four men who refused to stay still. Fill me with gumption, courage wrapped in common sense, and faith that You'll meet me in motion. Help me step forward even when the path isn't clear, trusting You to turn my small progression into Your big provision. Amen.

- Where in your life have you been "sitting at the gate," convinced there's no good move left?

- What's one bold, faith-filled action you can take today to show some gumption and move forward with God?

The *Joyful* Jab

Daily Bean 

"Weeping may endure for a night, but joy comes in the morning."
— **Psalms 30:5 (NIV)**

Sip of the Day

When was the last time you laughed — I mean, really laughed?
Not the polite, "that's cute" laugh, but the kind that makes your
shoulders drop and your soul breathe again. If it's been a minute,
this one's for you.

Psalm 30:5 isn't just a feel-good line; it's a promise. It reminds
us that tears are temporary and joy is guaranteed. God never
denies our pain — He refuses to let it have the final word. Every
night season has a morning, and joy is Heaven's proof that new
beginnings are always on the way.

Here's the truth: you can't say you trust God and keep walking
around hopeless, bitter, or permanently "over it." Real faith
doesn't erase hard things — it just finds joy right in the middle
of them. That's why the F in SELFIE stands for Finding Joy. It's
the habit of searching for God's goodness even when the scene
looks messy, choosing laughter over lament, and remembering
that joy isn't a reward — it's a rhythm.

Every time life throws a punch, shout "JOY!" When God makes a way, shout "JOY!" When things feel uncertain but you still sense His hand, shout "JOY!" Speaking joy isn't noise; it's spiritual warfare. It changes your atmosphere and reminds your heart who's still in charge.

Joy isn't the end of the fight — it's your stance while you're swinging. So today, find your rhythm, lift your head, and laugh like someone who already knows how this story ends. That's the joyful jab that knocks discouragement flat in your #BestSelfie Life.

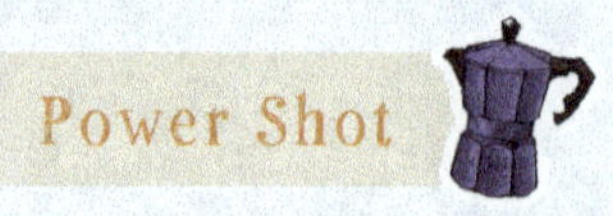

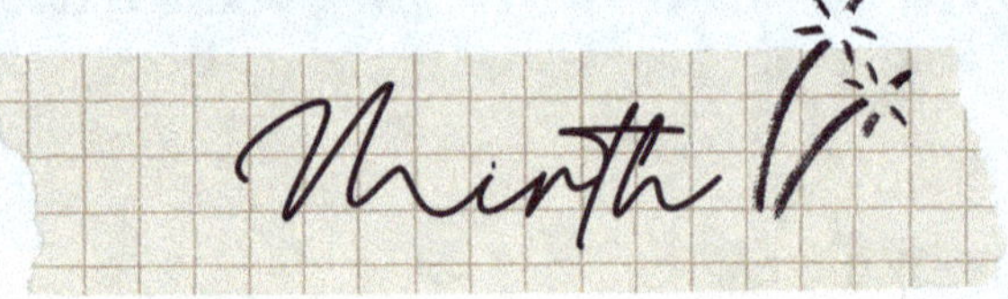

Mirth:
(murrth) noun

Definition: Great joy, amusement, or gladness, often expressed withlaughter.

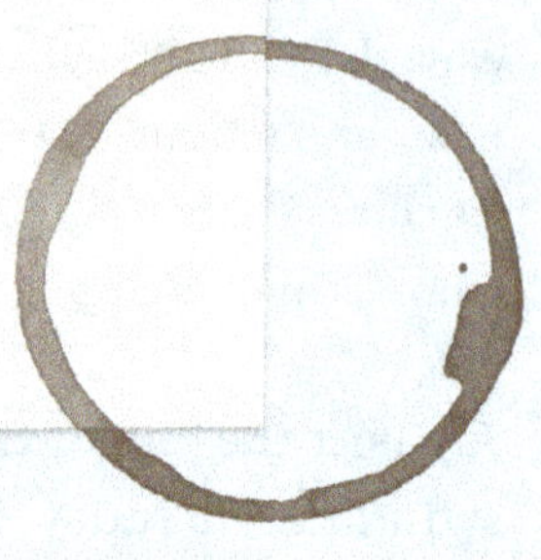

Rev Says

"Feeling gloomy, Selfie Superstar? Time to bring back your **mirth**! God's got your back, so lift that chin, take a breath, and let your joy show. Don't let life's jabs steal your laughter — laugh louder! That's faith with a grin."

God,
sometimes I let frustration steal my joy. Thank You for the promise that even when tears last for the night, Your joy is already on its way. Help me to live the "F" in SELFIE — Finding Joy in You, even in the middle of the mess. Fill me with mirth today, the kind that laughs, heals, and reminds me that You always bring the morning. Amen.

- What's one situation that's been making you pout, and how can you flip it into a reason to *shout 'JOY!'*?

- How can you intentionally bring mirth into your day — through gratitude, laughter, or celebration?

God's GPS

Daily Bean 

"Only acknowledge your guilt—you have rebelled against the Lord your God and have scattered your favors to foreign gods under every spreading tree and have not obeyed me,' declares the Lord. 'Return, faithless people,' declares the Lord, 'for I am your husband. I will choose one from a town and two from a clan and bring you to Zion.'" — *Jeremiah 3:13-14 (NIV)*

Sip of the Day

Sometimes we play a little game of Hide-and-Seek with God. Be honest, how many things do you quietly slide in front of Him? Your demanding job? Your adorable (but all-consuming) kids? That endless scroll of excuses? Or maybe your latest Netflix binge that turned "one episode" into "well... it's 2 a.m."

We say we're seeking Him, but most days we're just running in circles—busy, distracted, and spiritually out of breath.

And isn't it ironic how we ask God to *"order our steps,"* then get mad when He cancels a few of them? We say we trust His timing, but secretly want Him to co-sign *our* calendar. We claim we're waiting on direction, but if we're honest, we've been cruising in circles—spiritually adrift with the gas light on.

That's precisely what Jeremiah 3 captures. God's people drifted miles off course, chasing every shiny "foreign god," yet His response wasn't, "I'm done." It was "Return to Me." No punishment, just a patient invitation. The same grace applies to you, Selfie Superstar: God doesn't cut you off when you wander—He whispers, *"Re-route Me in."*

That's where today's tiny habit comes in:

The Whisper Habit, rooted in the I of SELFIE: Inhaling God's Peace and Presence. When life gets loud and you start drifting, don't shout over the chaos—*whisper through it.* Pause, take a deep breath, and quietly say, **"Re-route me, Lord."**

Whispering slows your soul. It quiets anxiety long enough for His presence to speak peace and give direction. Every whisper is a holy recalibration—inhale His calm, exhale control. You don't have to find the way; you just have to listen to the One who already knows it.

So, next time you catch yourself playing spiritual Hide-and-Seek, stop hiding behind hurry. Take a breath. Whisper your way home. God's GPS never loses signal; it's waiting for you to breathe in and believe again.

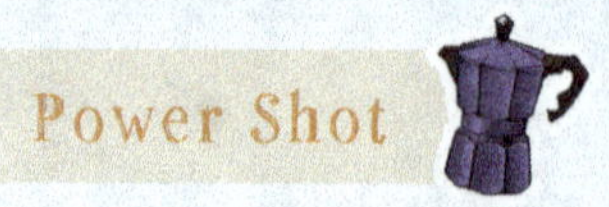

Adrift:
(uh-DRIFT) adjective/adverb

Definition: Without being steered or anchored; figuratively, lacking direction or purpose.

"You can't outrun grace, superstar! God's GPS doesn't freeze up just 'cause you got distracted. Stop the noise, take a breath, and whisper, 'Re-route me, Lord.' Watch how fast He pulls you back to peace."

Lord,
sometimes I chase everything but You and wonder why I feel lost. Thank You for never giving up, for always whispering me home. Teach me to inhale Your peace, exhale my plans, and trust Your steady direction. Re-route my steps toward Your perfect will and my #BestSelfie Life. Amen.

- What's one area of your life where you've been playing spiritual *Hide and Seek*—busy but secretly adrift?

- How can practicing the Whisper Habit help you inhale God's peace and bring you back to alignment today?

The *Divine* Download

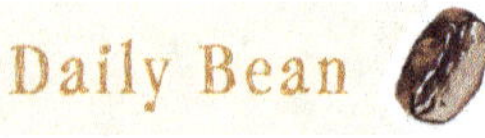

"And God is able to bless you abundantly, so that in all things at all times, having all that you need, you will abound in every good work." — **2 Corinthians 9:8 (NIV)**

Sip of the Day 

Confession time: I'm the type who likes to see the whole plan. I'll tell God, "I trust You," but then still refresh my email just in case He cc'd me on the blueprint. And yet, no matter how many spreadsheets or to-do lists I build, His provision still shows up in ways I never could've planned. Every single time.

That's what 2 Corinthians 9:8 is talking about—a divine download of abundance that keeps refreshing even when your signal feels weak. God isn't stingy. He doesn't trickle out blessings like a slow Wi-Fi connection; He floods your inbox with everything you need to do every good thing He's called you to do.

Here's the kicker: His downloads aren't just for your personal storage. They're meant to be shared. God doesn't fill your cup so you can hoard the coffee. He fills it so you can pour someone else a cup, too. The overflow isn't accidental; it's the assignment.

So, here's today's tiny habit:

The Download-Then-Do Habit, rooted in the E of SELFIE: Exhaling the illusion of control. Take a deep breath, slow the scroll, and ask yourself, "Who in my world could use a little overflow from my cup right now?"

Seriously, think about the last time you sensed God nudging you toward something—a conversation or a moment of generosity—and you brushed it off because you weren't sure it was the "right time." That's the thing about divine downloads: they rarely arrive on our schedule, but they always arrive on purpose.

Stay in the flow, superstar. Your cup was never meant to stay full; it was meant to stay pouring. That is how you live your #BestSelfie Life: open, generous, and completely in sync with God.

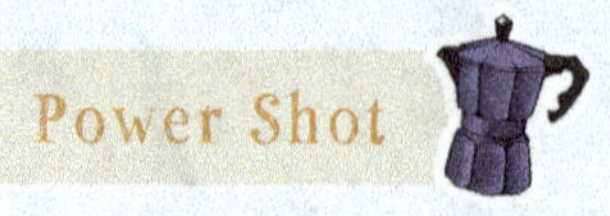

Magnanimous

Magnanimous:
(mag-NAN-uh-muhs) adjective

Definition: Generous or
forgiving, especially toward
a rival or someone less powerful.

"Listen, when God drops a
divine download, don't turn
into a data hoarder! He's been
magnanimous with you on
purpose. That blessing is not
meant to stop at your doorstep.
Pass it along, share the good
stuff, and watch how Heaven
keeps upgrading your plan
with unlimited grace!"

Dear God,
thank You for the divine
downloads that keep pouring into my life. Help me to stop waiting
for perfect clarity and move on the nudge You've already placed in my
heart. Forgive me for holding tight to what was meant to flow. Teach
me to exhale control, to live *magnanimously,* and to share my overflow
with others. Remind me that You never run out of grace to refill my cup.

Spill the Beans

- What's one download I've received lately that I haven't acted on yet?

- What small, magnanimous move could I make today to share what God's poured into me?

The Breakthrough Beat

Daily Bean

"About midnight, Paul and Silas were praying and singing hymns to God, and the other prisoners were listening to them. Suddenly, a violent earthquake shook the prison's foundations. At once all the prison doors flew open, and everyone's chains came loose."
— **Acts 16:25-26 (NIV)**

Sip of the Day

Confession time: sometimes when life falls apart, I want to grab my phone and text God something like, "Hey Lord, just circling back on that last prayer ... any ETA on the breakthrough?"

But Paul and Silas didn't text; they sang.

These two men were bruised, exhausted, and sitting in a jail cell that smelled like despair. Midnight hit, and instead of breaking down, they broke out in praise. No audience. No instruments. Just two believers turning a cellblock into a sanctuary. And then it happened—God moved. The floor quaked, the doors flew open, and every chain hit the ground.

Here's the truth: praise isn't a soundtrack; it's a strategy. It shifts your focus from fear to faith. It's what tells Heaven, "I'm still *trusting You*." Even in the dark, praise lights the match.

So here's your tiny habit:

The Midnight Melody Habit, tied to the F in SELFIE: Finding Joy in What Is. When pressure rises, hum your hope. Sing your gratitude. Whisper a lyric that reminds you who God is. Cue up your favorite worship song. You don't need perfect pitch, just a willing spirit. Every melody becomes a key that unlocks peace and invites joy back in.

Because sometimes the miracle doesn't begin with thunder; it begins with a tune. When your faith makes more noise than your fear, God steps into the situation and flips the night into morning.

So go on, lift that Breakthrough Beat. Let joy leak out of you until the atmosphere shifts. That's how freedom finds its way in.

Potency

Potency:
(POH-tuhn-see) noun

Definition: The power of something to influence or make an impression; effectiveness.

Rev Says

"Now hear me, praise isn't filler; it's fuel! That's the **potency** of your worship. When you open your mouth, Heaven opens doors. So sing like victory's already yours and let that Hallelujah shake the walls. Chains don't stand a chance against a believer with a melody and a little faith."

Lord,
thank You for the potency of praise. When life feels like midnight, teach me to hum my hope until peace returns. Let every note I lift silence fear and invite Your presence into the room. I believe my breakthrough is already in motion—for my #BestSelfie Life. Amen.

- Where in your life do you need God to break something open right now?

- How can you practice the Midnight Melody Habit today—singing, humming, or speaking joy when pressure hits?

The Endurance Test (You Got This!)

Daily Bean 

"You, however, know all about my teaching, my way of life, my purpose, faith, patience, love, endurance, persecutions, sufferings—what kinds of things happened to me in Antioch, Iconium, and Lystra, the persecutions I endured. Yet the Lord rescued me from all of them." — 2 Timothy 3:10-11 (NIV)

Sip of the Day

Let's not church it up; some days this faith walk feels like trying to run a marathon in heels. You love God, you're doing the work, you're saying all the right prayers... but life still hands you a test that makes you want to throw your coffee and crawl back under the covers.

Paul gets it. In this verse, he's telling Timothy, "I've been through it all—purpose, patience, pain, persecution—and guess what? God came through every single time." That's not a brag; it's a battle report from a man who refused to quit. Talk about a résumé! Paul wasn't just talking; he walked through life even when it was genuinely challenging.

Here's the truth: endurance isn't about pretending you're not tired. It's about choosing movement over meltdown. Trouble isn't proof that you're off track—it's confirmation that you're in training. The Lord doesn't waste a single ounce of your effort.

So here's your tiny habit:

The One More Step Habit, tied to the E in SELFIE: Exhaling what drains you. When your energy dips and everything in you wants to stop, take one more step. Then do one small thing that moves you forward, take the next step on your walk, finish that verse you were reading, or tidy the space around you. Every "one more step" builds spiritual muscle memory, teaching your faith to outlast your fatigue.

Because endurance isn't about speed, it's about staying in the race. Keep going. You're closer to the finish line than you think.

Keep going—you've got this, and God's got you.

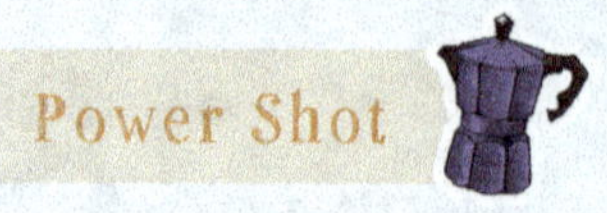

Indefatigable

Indefatigable:
(in-duh-FAT-i-guh-bul) adjective

Definition: (Of a person or their efforts) persisting tirelessly; incapable of being fatigued.

"Now that's what I call being **indefatigable**! When life turns up the heat, don't throw in the towel—just take one more step. You might slow down, but you don't stop. That's how God trains champions."

Lord,

I know living for You isn't always easy, and sometimes I want to give up. Thank You for reminding me that You'll rescue me from my troubles, just like You did for Paul. Help me stay indefatigable and keep going, no matter what comes my way. Amen.

- What specific challenge are you facing right now that's testing your endurance?

- How can you practice the One More Step Habit today, moving forward one faithful step at a time?

Your Next-Step *Strategy*

"The Lord makes firm the steps of the one who delights in him."
— **Psalm 37:23 (NIV)**

We've reached that sacred in-between place — the edge of what was and the start of what's next. Maybe you're standing still, wondering what direction to take. Perhaps you're already moving but not sure you're heading the right way. Here's the good news: none of it is wasted. **Every mile you've walked with God has been a masterclass in trust.**

Psalm 37:23 reminds us that God doesn't just bless the destination; He strengthens the steps. When you delight in Him, He builds your footing. Even when the path feels unclear, you can walk with quiet confidence knowing you're guided, guarded, and grounded.

Here's your tiny habit:

The Compass Check Habit. Once a day, pause before making a decision, replying to a message, or taking any other action, and ask, "Am I following His purpose or my preference?"

That one simple question can shift everything. It realigns your heart with Heaven's coordinates and keeps your internal compass calibrated toward peace, not pressure.

This habit ties to the S and L in SELFIE: *Stopping to look around.* Every time you practice it, you remind yourself that your journey is guided, not random. You're not wandering; you're walking in step with divine direction.

So today, check your compass. If your motives and your peace point north, keep going. The Lord is making your steps firm, and you're moving with purpose toward your #BestSelfie Life.

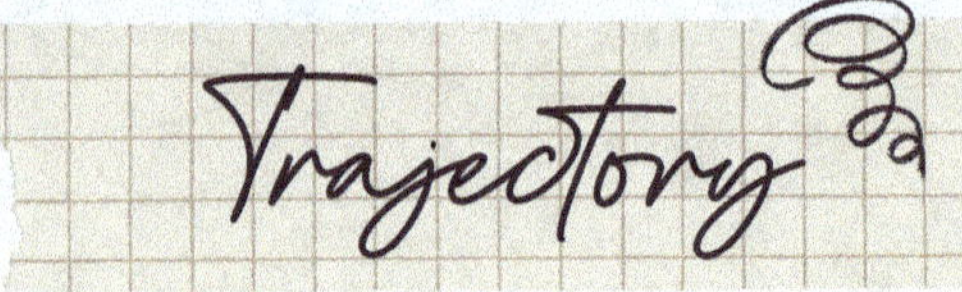

Trajectory

Trajectory:
(truh-JEK-tuh-ree) — noun

Definition: The path or progression
of something moving under a guiding
force or purpose.

"Life's a faith-walk, not a maze.
Don't get lost staring at the map
— check your compass! God's
already charted your **trajectory**,
and He's made you indefatigable
enough to keep going even when
the trail gets steep. So lift your
head, tighten those laces, and
keep moving. The view ahead?
Worth every step."

Lord,
thank You for being my true North.
Before I move, help me pause and check my compass.
Align my steps with Your purpose, not my preference.
Make my trajectory clear and my footing firm as I walk
into the next chapter of my #BestSelfie Life. Amen.

- What decision or direction in your life needs a *compass check* right now?

- How can you practice the Compass Check Habit today to make sure your next step points toward purpose, not preference?

The *Vision* *Board* Vibe

Daily Bean 

"Then the Lord replied: 'Write down the revelation and make it plain on tablets so that a herald may run with it. For the revelation awaits an appointed time; it speaks of the end and will not prove false. Though it linger, wait for it; it will certainly come and will not delay.'" — *Habakkuk 2:2-3 (NIV)*

Sip of the Day

You've reached the final cup in this 30-day journey — and what a pour it's been. Every devotion, every pause, every habit has been shaping the #BestSelfie version of you. You've learned to *sip smart* — to slow down, reflect deeply, and savor what God is doing one small step at a time.

Now it's time to dream forward. Habakkuk 2:2 isn't just good advice — it's God's creative call to action. "Write down the revelation and make it plain." Translation? Don't just think about your purpose; *put it on paper*. God's asking you to co-author your next chapter with Him.

Habit 30

Before this day ends, carve out time for your Believe List. On the following few pages, write down what you *believe* God will do next in your life — the promises He's whispered, the dreams He's planted, the unfinished business He's still perfecting. It's not a to-do list; it's a to-trust list.

And as you write, remember the F in SELFIE — *Finding joy in what is*. The vision board of your faith doesn't begin with "someday"; it starts with gratitude for *today*. Because when you delight in the now, you're perfectly positioned for what's next.

So sip slow, write bold, and make it plain. You're not done — you're just beginning another chapter of your *Unfinished Business*.

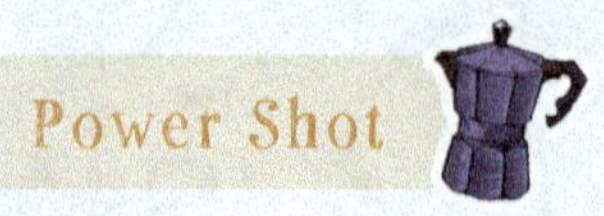

Clarity:
(KLAIR-i-tee) — noun

Definition: The quality of being clear, focused, and easy to understand; the state of seeing something as it truly is.

Rev Says 

"Vision without writing is just wishing. God said, 'Make it plain!' So jot it, plot it, and pray over it. When you write with **clarity**, you give your faith coordinates. Keep believing — your vision's already scheduled for delivery."

Lord,
thank You for the vision You've planted in me.
Help me write it down with faith, see it with clarity, and wait with joy.
As I sip smart and walk boldly into what's next, remind me that my story
is still unfolding — and every unfinished page is in Your hands. Amen.

- What dream, goal, or "unfinished business" needs to be written down today?

- How can you find joy in the waiting, trusting that God's appointed time is already in motion?

The Believe List

HABIT 29 EXTENDED

You've walked through 29 habits that reshaped
your mindset, faith, and daily rhythm.

Now it's time to declare what you believe
for the next season of your life.

Think of this page as your personal prayer wall in
book form — the place where you put faith into ink.

What unfinished business
is still stirring in your spirit?

What dreams are you trusting God to complete?

What steps will require courage,
consistency, and commitment from you?

As you write your Believe List, don't edit your hope.

Be bold like Jabez and ask big.

Pray with confidence.

Trust that what you put on paper is
already known in Heaven.

"The Lord makes firm the steps of the one
who delights in him."— **Psalm 37:23 NIV**

My Believe List

(WHAT I'M TRUSTING GOD TO FINISH, FULFILL,
OR REFINE IN MY #BESTSELFIE LIFE)

1. ○
2. ○
3. ○
4. ○
5. ○
6. ○
7. ○
8. ○
9. ○
10. ○
11. ○
12. ○
13. ○
14. ○
15. ○
16. ○
17. ○
18. ○
19. ○
20. ○

"Faith is the evidence of things hoped for." — **Hebrews 11:1**

A free space for creativity,
reflection, or inspiration.

"Brothers and sisters, I do not consider myself yet to have taken hold of it.

But one thing I do: forgetting what is behind and straining toward what is ahead,

I press on toward the goal to win the prize for which God has called me heavenward in Christ Jesus."
— **Philippians 3:13-14 (NIV)**

Hey friend,

Look at us, still standing, still sipping, still becoming. We made it to the end, and yet this isn't really "the end." It's that satisfying sip before you refill your cup and keep going.

Every page of this journey was written from the same space you're in right now, somewhere between not yet and almost there. There were days I doubted, cried, nights I prayed, and mornings I rewrote every line with a full heart. In those moments, I heard God whisper, "You're unfinished on purpose."

As someone who lives with perfectionism, I've learned through this journey that being unfinished isn't a flaw; it's faith in motion. It means we're still learning to sip smart, to pause when needed, and to trust God with the middle parts of our story, the ones that don't fit neatly into an Instagram caption.

Rev would remind you to keep that faith mug full and your hope hotter than your morning coffee. He'd tell you that progress is sacred, even when it's slow. And Paws? He'd probably wag, curl up, and prove that peace often looks like presence.

So, here's our prayer for you: keep pressing forward, not perfectly, but purposefully. Keep showing up with courage. Keep pouring love into your world. And when life feels unfinished —because it will —remember that's precisely where grace does its best work.

Thank you for walking this 30-day journey with us. From our hearts (and paws) to yours: keep sipping, keep shining, and keep becoming the masterpiece God's still painting.

With love,
Dr. Shan,
Rev + Paws

Sip slowly. Pray bold. Live unfinished.

(The story isn't over, just brewing.)

www.ingramcontent.com/pod-product-compliance
Lightning Source LLC
Chambersburg PA
CBHW071437130726
47997CB00006B/2128